About the Author

Raised in Southern California, the author now resides in the rural mountain community of Quincy, in the center of the California Sierra-Nevada Range. His training includes a Ph.D. from the University of Wisconsin-Milwaukee and an internship in Community and Clinical Psychology from the University of Kansas Medical School. Dr. Mac has worked with community mental health centers in family counseling and provided various treatment programs and workshops for the past ten years where he counseled hundreds of families using his child-rearing concepts.

In addition to teaching classes in child-rearing and providing consultation to probation officers and child protective workers he organized several group homes for delinquent and neglected adolescents. Dr. Mac is on a regional board serving the mentally retarded and developmentally disabled.

Other professional interests include developing an employee assistance program for lumber mill workers, being active in alcoholism and drug treatment programs, and giving workshops in stress management and the use of biofeedback.

In his leisure the author enjoys white water rafting, skiing, and wilderness trips with his wife. Nancy Mac is a commercial artist currently employed by the U.S. Forest Service.

CHILD-REARING: WHAT TO DO NOW

CHILD-REARING: WHAT TO DO NOW

by
Roddy Mac, Ph.D.

Published by
Med-Psych Publications

Pine Mountain Press, Inc. Publishing Group
P.O. Box 13604
Wauwatosa, WI 53226

CREDITS

Editor: *Marilyn A. Brilliant, M.S.*
Typesetting: *The Graphic Worx, ltd.*
Production & Printing: *ARCATA*

Acknowledgements

The author wishes to recognize Burton Deming, Ph.D. and Dorean Bouska, MSW for their kindly guidance into the field of child-rearing. He also thanks Avery Weeks for his encouragement in completing this work.

© 1984 by Roddy Mac

Manufactured in USA.

ISBN: 0-89769-079-6

Dedication

This book is dedicated to parents who want freedom to explore alternatives and have determination to do a better job.

TABLE OF CONTENTS

CHAPTER 1
WHAT MATTERS IN CHILD-REARING?

Child Rearing: What To Do Now

What Matters in Child-Rearing?

Controversy abounds in child-rearing policies and practices. Experts disagree and have disagreed for generations. Part of the disagreement stems from what each parent or expert believes is important. Each of our values and goals are slightly different and therefore what is important will be different.

While this book presents a general set of values my intent is not to convince you to adopt those exact values. The real importance of this book lies in offering a spectrum of child-rearing tools so that you may raise your child as you choose.

The techniques and approaches discussed are not new and revolutionary. They have stood the tests of time and assaults by rebellious children. The worth of the selected techniques and approaches is that they accomplish attitude and behavior change in children. My goal was to show you how to apply the techniques in a practical, down-to-earth way.

The plan for the next few pages in this Chapter is to select a variety of broad child-rearing goals. Probably you are already working toward them. Chapter 2 presents ten techniques; these are the tools of the trade. Chapter 3 reviews each child-rearing goal, showing how and when to use the ten techniques.

Chapters 4 and 5 examine frequently occurring parenting problems and how to solve them. In Chapter 6 there are strategies to deal with long-term or enduring life patterns. And Chapter 7 identifies parenting pitfalls and how to overcome them. Chapter 8 states guidelines which help identify particular concepts to use at certain ages, a developmental schedule. Chapter 9 offers suggestions regarding a child's education, at home and in school.

Goals for Children

I asked groups of parents to identify what they felt were important goals for their children. By listing parents' responses I filled a large blackboard with healthy, respectable qualities or traits. You may want to identify the traits you like to see in your children and compare your list with mine.

I grouped the list into a manageable number of broad categories. For example, traits such as:

doing tasks without being reminded
paying bills
keeping appointments
being reliable
being on time
doing one's share
meeting obligations

were all grouped into the category of *Being Responsible* . Individual goals of:

being confident
independent

14

assertive
sticking up for one's self
not needing drugs or alcohol to feel good
were all grouped into the category of *Feeling Good About Oneself*.
    I reduced the list to four major categories. Those categories were:
    1. Being Responsible
    2. Feeling Good About Oneself
    3. Likable
    4. Communicates Well
    Remember, these categories represent a broad range of specific goals or traits. The *Likable* category includes such traits as:
    warmth
    respect toward others
    caring
    generous
    agreeable
    pleasant
    willing to make compromise
    having a sense of humor
    The *Communicates Well* category contains such goals as:
    understands self and others
    describes how self and others feel
    easy to talk to
    a good listener
    The task now is to develop a child-rearing policy which will result in the desired end-products, a child who rates high in these qualities. While it appears to be an ambitious task, and is, it is a task which parents never-

theless set out to do anyway.

Help for Parents

Part of the challenge in developing a child-rearing policy is to make the job easier on you, the parent. You have certain needs. A difficult, cumbersome, complicated, and time consuming scheme is not going to meet your needs.

I believe that making full use of the tools and concepts in this book will allow you to:

Reduce the time spent in punishing, screaming and arguing.

Increase the time spent in praising and playing with your child(ren).

Reduce your responsibilities by having your kids assume more responsibilities.

Utilize the least harsh punishment which will effectively do the job.

Develop a whole program that makes sense and is logical enough so deciding what to do will be an easy matter.

Most parents I see in counseling actually put in more time doing things the wrong way than it would take to do it right. Often this is because parents simply repeat their mistakes. They don't see any alternative but to try harder — in the wrong direction once again. By having the alternatives of several good approaches to a problem you can make your job more fun and less drudgery.

CHAPTER 2.
TEN TECHNIQUES

Child Rearing: What To Do Now

Ten Techniques

Let's suppose you were to try playing golf with only one club. A round of golf would be much more difficult. The game would take longer to finish and probably would be less enjoyable. Of course, deciding on which club to choose would be an easy matter. You would always reach for the same one, sometimes using the club to its best advantage and more often cursing its ineffectiveness. Rather than look for other clubs to use you might blame the course or yourself for being a failure. Eventually you would finish, just as each parent will complete their role. Yet, you would have performed far better at both tasks if you began with a full set of alternatives and knew how to use each well.

Here are ten techniques which provide you with the alternatives you need for child-rearing. They are the building blocks, practical, time-tested tools which help guide you in the difficult role of parenting. The ten tech-

niques are:
1. Modeling
2. Trial-and-error
3. Rules
4. Ignoring
5. Consequences
6. Love
7. Humor
8. Reflective Listening
9. Saving Face
10. Negotiation

None of these techniques are ends in themselves. They are the methods by which you guide your child toward goals of your choosing. Keep in mind that you don't have to pick the "perfect" technique every time. Several of the techniques could be used to accomplish the task at hand. Likewise, there are several techniques you wouldn't want to use on a given task. There is nothing mysterious in this. For example, I have used a screwdriver for many purposes besides driving a screw. Some uses were brilliant (after a fashion) while other uses had me scurrying to the hardware store to replace the screwdriver I ruined. Fortunately, you can afford lots of mistakes in child-rearing without doing irreparable harm. The key is to evaluate your technique and switch to another if one is not working well.

Note to readers: This book becomes more valuable if you continue to use it as a reference source. There is really more material presented than normal parents can remember in a single reading.

1. Modeling

Ten Techniques

Modeling or imitation is a simple and powerful tool. It means if you want your child to act a certain way then act that way yourself. It is such a simple, common occurrence that you can easily forget its value. As with any of the techniques it is not 100% effective. Just because you make your bed each morning doesn't mean your son will follow suit. Nevertheless, he is much more likely to adopt the habit if you make your bed than if you don't.

Current research suggests that modeling is an effective technique in teaching children how to show emotions. For example, if you fight with your spouse, avoid arguments, yell, laugh, sulk, cry, drink, or throw temper tantrums your children are likely to use the same behaviors to express their emotions. Each of us are taught how to show our feelings partially by how "significant" others (parents) show feelings.

As with anything, modeling can be overdone. If you adopt the "watch what I do; learn by what I do" policy it can result in your kids sitting back and letting you do all the work. Probably the most influential type of modeling is the type that takes place daily. It is your day-to-day style of life which provides the most impact. What you usually do under stress, tension, when criticized, when you are studious, industrious, playful, or affectionate is what is picked up by your children and imitated. Modeling is a significant contributor to each of the four general goals for children mentioned in Chapter 1.

One aspect of the modeling technique is that it provides you with feedback about yourself. See yourself in your child as the child imitates you. If you don't like your child's attitude (negativism or know-it-all nature) look in a mirror to discover the cause. A stubborn parent begets a stubborn child; a gentle parent usually prides in a gentle sire.

2. Trial-and error

This technique means that we all "tend" to learn from our successes and failures. First-hand experiences can be an excellent teacher. Experience can also be unforgiving so you need to guard against disasterous consequences. Still, there is a great benefit in letting your child go to school in winter without his coat. It doesn't mean the youngster will remember this lesson the first time. It may take several trials. Fortunately, most children do learn from their experiences. At times it may not seem like it though.

If you watch a young child you can actually see the process of trial-and-error. The child will explore the environment. In the process of exploration some activities will be punished and others rewarded naturally. If he pulls the cat's tail it might scratch — a punishment. If a ball is rolled and makes interesting noises the child is rewarded. Your child does not need to see you pull the cat's tail or roll the ball (modeling). It is the trial-and-error process that is responsible for throwing temper tantrums in public and whining. By the same process your child can just as easily learn to behave acceptably, if he meets with reward or pleasure for acceptable behavior.

The hallmark of this technique is that you can take a back seat and let nature take its course. Forewarnings and I-told-you-so's only detract from this technique. Repetition is very important in this learning process. Trial-and-error is useful because nature does the punishing — not you. You may serve as a listening post or even give condolences to your child. The learning has taken place without your direct interventions.

An overprotective parent underutilizes this technique while a neglectful parent overuses it. It is a powerful tool when developing a child's sense of confidence and independence. It's also a leading contributor to fostering the general goal of *Being Responsible* and to some extent *Feeling Good About Oneself*.

3. Rules

This technique delegates responsibility to children. As used here it has a very specific meaning. In order to use the rule setting approach you must accomplish the following:

1. Define what is expected in very precise and detailed language.
2. The results need to be clearly and easily observable.
3. A consequence (the positive or negative) is established at the *beginning* for complying or not complying with the rule.
4. There is a time or event limit that "automatically" triggers the consequence.
5. Rules are in force over long periods of time.
6. A consequence is chosen, keeping in mind that the child is expected to "test" or break the rule on a number of occasions. Don't make the consequence too harsh.

Any of the above items, if eliminated, will seriously reduce the effectiveness of this technique. The method of setting rules should be limited in several ways. Only a small number of rules, such as chores, should be maintained at any one time. Introduce one rule at a time and wait until it is being regularly accomplished before introducing another. This one-at-a-time approach maximizes success and is less burdensome for you to enforce. Rules should only be reserved for frequently appearing problems. Setting a rule is time consuming; yet, if you devote the extra time in the beginning it will drastically reduce conflicts and aggravation.

The technique of rules is very effective for chores. Teaching responsibility through use of rules will take years. So be pateint. Avoid allowing too many exceptions or excuses for not complying with each rule, especially early in the process. Being rigid about rules can be balanced with leniency in other areas.

4. Ignoring

Ignoring means not paying attention to a youngster. It involves withdrawing *all* the typical forms of recognition such as seeing, hearing, and touching. Here is an approach where turning your back on a situation may actually improve things.

As a technique, ignoring is different from punishment. Sometimes it is called a "time-out" from positive reinforcement or attention. It works because children need your attention. When that attention is withdrawn your child will gradually (or sometimes abruptly) stop the undesirable behavior. The effect usually is for the child to switch to acceptable behavior in order to regain your prized attention. None of us like to be ignored. When used selectively and on specific behaviors it can be far more effective than a spanking or a harsh word.

The value of ignoring depends upon its wise and discriminative use. It can be used in situations where your child or teenager is trying to secure your attention inappropriately. Situations such as temper tantrums, showing off, demands, nagging or whining are good opportunities to employ the ignoring technique. Slight variations include sending the child to his room or the old sit-in-the-corner isolation. Often it is not necessary to maintain ignoring for long periods of time. A brief few minutes is often powerful enough to get the point across. Basically, you are establishing a separation between you and your child. This separation allows the child to alter his behavior and still save face if he chooses to do so.

The trial-and-error learning process showed how your child can learn an undesireable or desireable behavior. The ignoring tool is a device to influence that choice. Your attention serves to reward or punish what you like to see repeated (desireable) or want stopped (undesireable).

The ignoring technique is probably the most frequently misused technique of all. Why? What do you think will happen if you ignore your quietly working child and pay attention, even negative attention, to him when he is misbehaving? Or, what will happen when you ignore his demands for a while, then finally give in to those demands? What will happen if you ignore dirty words sometimes and sometimes you pay attention to the language? The answers suggest that you can teach healthy activities or can promote misbehavior, nagging persistance and profanity. You use the technique of ignoring often, daily, even though you are not aware you're using it. Now, you can be aware of the technique and use it to accomplish your goals.

5. Consequences

The idea that there should be some judgment rendered to a wayward child is familiar and acceptable to most parents. A common term is "punishment". Yet, punishment is a narrow view of the technique of using consequences. As applied here, consequences mean *anything* that comes after a child's behavior that is used to stop or encourage the behavior. Ignoring is a special case of using consequences as is the technique of humor, discussed later. Setting rules also incorporates a consequence for complying or not complying with what is expected.

The technique of consequences covers many general uses. One value in using this technique is in having your child take responsibility for her actions. The process is best employed when the consequence is having your child clean up after herself, replace the broken object or pay for the damages. If she makes a mess, having her clean it up is more fitting and easier on you than meting out additional punishment. The purpose is to allow her to explore her environment to the fullest while encouraging her to be responsible for her actions.

A second way to apply consequences is by encouraging desired behavior. If ignoring is used to eliminate behavior then paying attention to the child should encourage other behavior. It does! The consequences here may be a touch, a smile, a nod, a few words of praise, or playing with your child. Those positive consequences can be employed to reward good or desired behavior such as independent work, persistence, cooperative play or helping out.

Other uses for consequences include showing displeasure (a frown, saying you're disappointed, or a swift slap) when the child really should have known better. The essence of the technique is to have it come *immediately* after the behavior, set a *moderate strength* consequence, try to have the consequence *fit* the offense, and depend upon *repetition* to do the teaching.

There are different types of consequences. The form in most trial-and-error procedures is a naturally occurring consequence. Touching a hot stove, fingers on live electric wires, falling off a precarious perch, breaking a neighbor's window, forgetting a jacket, leaving something out where it can be stolen, and neglecting to put needed clothes in the wash, all result in a "natural" consequence. If you do not interfere, these naturally occurring consequences will do the teaching for you. Fight against your impulse to protect, guide and prevent these excellent natural teaching devices.

Setting rules often involves consequences you establish or impose. A privilege is granted or taken away. Try to pick a consequence that makes sense. For example, for a rule about playing a record player or TV too loud, a consequence of being grounded or not allowing a friend to visit, makes less sense than immediately turning the machine off for a specified length of time. Ask yourself if the consequence logically follows the rule. Fit the punishment or reward to the act as closely as you can.

Note to readers: This is the half-way point in explaining the ten basic techniques. The five already covered tend to be rather aggressive tools. They are active ways to alter behavior. The following five, as a group, are less direct, more personable tools, often shaping attitudes and social interaction. This is not to say that the next five techniques are less powerful. They are just as strong, but the visible effects may be less immediate. These next five methods operate on the internal dynamics of children such as feelings of security, self-worth, and sense of well being.

6. Love

It may sound strange to say "love" is a technique, but love is a powerful, necessary, and often neglected tool. As with the other techniques this tool can be used improperly, either too infrequently, overly used, or used at the wrong times. Does showing love come naturally to you? For many parents it doesn't feel natural or they feel loving but find it difficult to openly and frequently express the love.

Most of the other techniques are *conditional*. Something happens as a result of or a condition of your child's behavior. The techniques of love is *unconditional;* it is given without your child having accomplished anything. Surprisingly, giving unconditional love is perhaps the least well understood, least researched, of these techniques. The tool is employed in building good feelings about oneself. Unconditional love builds an inner security that youngsters use to combat and reject harmful peer pressure and the abuse of alcohol or drugs. It is important to feel good not only because we perform a task well, but for just being (ourselves). This fosters a reasonable and necessary amount of self-satisfaction and contentment.

We can speculate that if you wanted to produce a striving, restless and never fully satisfied youngster, then giving unconditional love would not be the best tool. Showing only conditional love, love shown when your child accomplished a desired task, teaches him that he is only valued for his accomplishments. Thus, he learns to accomplish more. Therefore, it is a value judgement you must make on how much unconditional love is sufficient and helpful. It is my feeling that showing lots of unconditional love serves to produce a more healthy, happy individual.

Show love by touching, hugging, smiling, verbally stating appreciation, and doing something to show love and concern. Unfortunately, there are no norms or guidelines to follow on how frequent you should show love. Some children appear to manage on remarkably little love. I suppose it is possible to smother your child in too much unconditional love. It would take an awful lot though. It is difficult for most parents to provide enough unconditional love so as to offset all those sarcastic, demeaning, and critical remarks parents make but don't mean. Have you ever heard of anyone complaining that their mother or father told them too many (unconditionally) good compliments? I haven't.

I have heard complaints of excessive conditional love. It can seem like a manipulative pressure to coerce compliance. Sometimes it is used to enslave. Unconditional love is the method you will want to practice.

7. Humor
This technique is also not typically thought of as a child-rearing tool. And, as with the technique of love, it is not well understood.

Examples of humor include: laughing, smiling, playing a game, teaching, laughing at oneself, being carefree, and making a joke out of some situation. Obviously, abusing this technique is possible, particularly when teasing or making fun of someone.

Humor brings relief to a stressful situation. It teaches humility by being able to laugh at yourself. Humor creates a light, warm home life. The joy of having kids is that it can be fun. Humor is not ridicule; it is something positive for both you and your child. If your child is not comfortable with or is not laughing at your humor then you're not using the approach correctly. Humor is in the eyes of the beholder, the receiver.

With older kids especially, humor injected at yourself can reduce tension and make negotiations easier. When there is irreconcilable differences between what your child wants and what you will allow, then humor serves to ease the conflict. Saying with a comforting smile (not sarcastically), "Sometimes, son, your father is more stubborn than his son;" or "Maybe you're right. I'm so old fashion that you could sell me as an antique and make a fortune," are ways to allow your child to save face while still not agreeing with him. Common subjects which produce unresolvable (at least for the time being) conflict are playmates, dating, dress, hair length, degree of freedom, and access to the family car. If done properly a smile of disagreement, with humor, effectively ends the immediate argument.

Following a disagreement on political figures, Dad says "OK son, you win this round." This father effectively showed his son a warm, caring smile along with the words. The son went away feeling father heard him, even though he wasn't able to change the old man's opinion. Dad successfully ended this discussion allowing his son to save face while disagreeing with the boy's ideas.

The smile in the above example was not sarcastic or

teasing. The humor of saying, "You win this round" doesn't mean the father agrees. It means that the father wants to end the discussion on a lighter note. It is a mild way of acknowledging an unresolvable difference. Basically, if father is able to show a genuine, warm smile along with the friendliness of humor he will find it difficult to be totally upset with his son. Humor can end hostility and show acceptance of the person, not necessarily acceptance of the ideas the person has. In addition, father is being a good model. The son learns through modeling or imitation that differences are not necessarily heavy, unhappy events to avoid, or fight over. Humor and smiles are more catching than a cold. Pleasantness is infectious.

8. Reflective Listening

Reflective listening is a skill; it lies at the heart of communicating. This skill involves careful listening so you can put yourself in your child's shoes. The other vital part is to reflect or state a summary of what you heard your child say. If successfully employed it demonstrates that you clearly understand what is said or implied. By using reflective listening you can communicate without giving your opinion or taking a stand. Withholding your opinion is extremely valuable when you want to teach your child how to solve his own problem. You can be a good sounding board; you can help clarify the child's often fuzzy, inarticulate thoughts; and you can encourage closeness by understanding without directing. You show understanding by practicing the technique of reflective listening.

The process of reflective listening is easy to describe and appears simple, but I have found it difficult for people

31

to actually use. Fundamentally, the idea is to put your child's words and feelings into a clear statement. Mirror the statement back to her. The reflected message describes, clarifies, and verifies what she is saying to you. Therefore, the mirroring must reflect a good image; it must describe her ideas in an accurate and logical fashion.

It is helpful to go a step beyond the simple rendering. Make the mirror a beautiful, magic one. By taking your child's fuzzy, immature, or incomplete thought and reflecting back a more complete statement, which puts her in a good light, the mirror becomes a magical aid. It helps her to learn the right words to describe feelings. By not distorting her feelings you will have helped her to communicate with you more accurately. You'll also find that she will enjoy talking with you because she will feel that you "understand" her.

What does reflective listening do? The benefits of skillfully using reflective listening are enormous. Below are some of the benefits derived from judicious practice of the technique:

1. You can verify what you thought your child said. Is it what she intended to say?
2. It gives her an unrushed turn to be really heard.
3. It can provide her with more precise language with which to express ideas and feelings.
4. It makes her feel that her parents respect her.
5. It keeps everyone focusing on the subject rather than drifting away to other matters.
6. It allows you to reserve judgement until you hear the entire issue.
7. It tells her that although her parents will listen they

---

may not solve the problem for her.
8. Even if she doesn't get her way it leaves both sides feeling better about each other (i.e., respect and honor for each other).

Reflective listening could and probably should be used daily. To take full advantage of this technique it must be practiced. Reflecting is a skill that needs to be in constant use. Most people feel awkward when first trying reflecting. They feel silly and complain that the conversation bogs down. After a while it becomes much easier and conversation flows.

In marital counseling I have used a simple game to encourage the skill. The idea is to have one person take a turn. That person holds some symbol such as a pencil, pillow or crown. While the speaker has possession of the pencil he can talk about whatever he wants. The listener must win the pencil. The listener does this by correctly reflecting. When the speaker declares that the listener understood then he gives the listener the pencil. Now it's the other side's turn to answer or offer an opinion. The judge of whether or not the listener correctly understood is the speaker.

Several things become obvious when playing the game with a new couple. First, the speaker needs to keep statements brief. If the statement is long-winded the listener can't hope to reflect all that is said. Also, it is amazing how difficult it is for the listener to hold his tongue until the speaker finishes. The listener usually is so impatient that he can hardly wait for the speaker to finish before barging in. The listener may need to be reminded that he cannot answer until after accurately reflecting the speaker's statement.

With children, particularly young children, this game is difficult to play. Young children need to learn the skill from parents modeling the technique. You can ask your young child, "Now, what did I say; What do you think I am saying to you; Tell me what I said; or, Tell me what I said so I can be sure you understand me."

Parents need to bear in mind that understanding what your child is saying or feeling does not mean you agree or approve. First, you must understand; then, if required or requested you can give an opinion or judgement. A very common complaint teens have is that their parents do not "understand" them; they can't "talk" with their parents. The reason for this feeling is that parents do not try to understand; they just tell the kids what to do. Sure, it's for the child's own benefit and parents really do want the best for their children, but kids need to be understood regardless of whether they are right or wrong.

It might be that parents accurately understand, yet the missing element is that parents fail to restate that understanding. Unless parents actually verbalize the youngster's position the child continues to doubt that the parent understands. Kids reject parents when parents always have answers. Kids need understanding more than directions, particularly older kids. A simple answer for why the "generation gap" is that reflective listening is not employed.

The technique of reflecting is particularly needed when:

1. It's the child's responsibility to do something about a problem. You help out by serving as a listening post.
2. Your child wants to have you understand something, but not take action.

3. You want your child to confide in you and turn to you for help in embarrassing situations.

9. Saving Face

Some techniques such as rule setting, consequences, and ignoring tend to be unconcerned with children's feelings. For example, children don't have to like doing dishes, making beds or saying "Please"; they just need to comply. Here is a technique which is exclusively concerned with children's feelings. There are times when more progress can be made by allowing your child to save face than by using direct force. There are many ways to implement the technique of saving face. A parent uses the technique by allowing a measure of self-determination, avoiding publicizing guilt, and as a tension reducer.

Allowing a child a measure of self-determination is shown by giving the child choices. "I need your help. You can help me now or during the TV commercial." Variations are: after the movie or show, at the end of that game, or in five minutes. If your child selects the delay, wait until the deadline. If she voluntarily remembers, you have a pleasant success. If you get no voluntary response it's not a failure, rather it means you still have a way to go. The best way to handle "forgetting" in this instance is to wait a few moments to see if she responds then say, "The commercial is on." You are again employing the saving face technique by allowing your child additional time to comply with your request. If the child helps you after your reminder you've scored a partial success. If there's still no sign of compliance you may need to take other action. (For example, the technique of consequences could be used — turn off the TV.) Nevertheless, your actions were designed to maximize a child's sense of control, within limits. When allowing the extra time period always be sure to return at the deadline. If you usually forget, your child will also learn to forget.

Another application of self-determination is to allow your child to do something you know will not work. The child will try it and find out it doesn't work. Your role is to determine whether it is safe for her to fail, to support the eagerness for exploration by giving permission, avoid making a doomsday prediction of failure, and refrain from saying, "I told you so," or "I knew it wouldn't work."

When you avoid publicizing your child's guilt you employ saving face. Publicity means forcing a confession. What is the purpose of forcing a confession out of a child, especially when you may already know the truth? A mistake may be made when you follow the line of logic: "I want to teach my child to be truthful. I want her to know that it will be better for her to tell me the truth than to lie." While that may sound logical it can actually force your child into a lie. A child, frightened and cornered, may try to escape with a lie. Don't continue to frighten her by saying it will go easier for her if she "owns up" to the truth. It is not to your advantage to scare a confession out of her. If she hasn't already (immediately) confessed, proceed to the appropriate consequence. The consequence selected should fit the guidelines given under the section on consequences.

People who handle animals regularly, know that most animals, even quite tame ones, when cornered become aggressive. When you "corner" your child, the child tends to produce undesirable behavior. She may tell a lie or deny the truth when confronted. "No, I didn't take the money," she says when you know full well that she did. "I didn't do it!" is a likely response when she feels threatened.

You may want to find out "Why" your child misbehaved. Ask yourself if you really are curious. If the curiosity is mixed with anger wait until the anger subsides before asking "Why" questions. If it's a matter of curiosity you should avoid using a loud, confrontive voice. Showing anger often serves to scare a child away from feeling guilty and into a defensive or denial stand. You want to allow room for guilt (and a child's natural desire to tell the truth) to work.

Finally, the technique of saving face is employed as a good tension reducer. Say, "I know you feel strongly; I can see it's important to you," or "You have a strong point there." Those statements do not mean you agree; in fact, it may mean you disagree with your child. These are tension reducing, face saving examples which can be used in the midst of conflict. This non-critical technique of acknowledging the child's logic, sincerity, and intensity of feeling makes you someone your child likes to talk to, despite your disagreement.

Just as there are many ways to use saving face there are likewise many benefits. Applying the technique automatically means you are trying to be courteous, polite and respectful as opposed to nagging, intimidating or embarrassing. Rather than degrading your child, you are giving them dignity. You're letting a child's conscience and sense of guilt fester, finally yielding a voluntary confession. You are approaching child-rearing by using diplomacy. Politicians know there are other methods besides diplomacy, yet the modern world uses diplomacy because it wins the respect and allegiance of others. You also want to win your child's respect while still getting the job done. The technique of saving face works by influencing through kindness, tolerance and acceptance.

10. Negotiation

Negotiation is essentially a procedure for resolving conflict. Other techniques (rules, ignoring, and consequences) are also for conflict resolution. But, in this decision-making technique you and your child are more equal participants. You choose to give up some authority in order to have your child assume some responsibility. The type of responsibility you want for her to assume is that she defines the conflict and suggests solutions for which both sides would agree. If you propose the final solution each time, then she is not learning to find compromises (solutions).

The value of this technique is in teaching real-life problem-solving techniques. It transfers half the burden to kids for resolving a multitude of differences between them and you. If your child is active in proposing and negotiating a solution, she is more likely to comply with her part of the bargain. With this approach you must be willing to give up certain things for other things. You give up total control and settle for a negotiated settlement in which both of you find reasonable and acceptable. Some authors have described this procedure as a "no lose" method because both sides get part of what they want.

The procedure of negotiation is a difficult one for most parents because it runs against the traditional custom of parental authority. Employers sometimes find that their employees are more satisfied and produce more work if employees have something to say about the job. Parents can use the same logic and methods without feeling insulted or weak. Keep in mind that the technique of negotiation is one alternative tool, not the only tool. It is my belief, though, that if you and your child learn the process of negotiation it will be a practice you use frequently. It is an enjoyable child-rearing tool.

Negotiating is time consuming; it is quicker to just say "no" or "yes" than discuss the problem. A simple example of your child wanting to go to the movie may involve many separate issues. You may say "no" because of the cost, the type of film, the peers going or transportation problems. You can exert your authority by making the decision. Yet, if the negotiation tool is utilized, your child might pleasantly overcome your prime objection(s) by possibly paying for the movie, going to another film, going with a different friend, having a chaperone, or arrange other transportation. Each side may get substantially what they want through the negotiating process.

Another example of how negotiation can be used is when your son wants to change his bed time. Rather than say "yes" or "no" go through the negotiation procedure. The basic elements are these:

1. Your child's wants and desires are clearly stated.
2. Your concerns of safety, convenience to you, and your basic desires are accurately stated.
3. Areas of agreement are identified.
4. Areas of disagreement are identified.
5. Propose solutions.
6. Compromise.
7. Try it.
8. Modify if necessary.

By having your son announcing his wants, a later bedtime, the first step is made. You may want to find out why he wants a later bedtime but it is not necessary to question him at length about it. Next, try to have him guess what your concerns are. You might say, "How do you think that will affect me?" Or, "Why should I be concerned about the change?" If your child does not guess your concerns then tell him what they are. The concerns could be about oversleeping in the morning, the difficulty in getting him to go to sleep already, or the extra noise he might make when you are wanting peace and quiet.

You may proceed by identifying the areas you both agree upon. You may both agree "in principal" to him being old enough to have a later bed time. You can even say that if your concerns were met that the change is possible. Your approval is conditional; it depends upon resolving the specific concerns you have. This positive approach will usually have your child trying to find a way of convincing you. Great! If he can solve your concerns, then why not let him try it to see if it will work.

The areas of disagreement may need to be identified in great detail. Repeat several times and if possible in different words exactly what items are in contention. Have your child state the disagreement from both sides. You may need to model by stating both positions yourself.

Your areas of disagreement on bed-time may be the exact time in his room or when lights are off. The disagreement may center around what to do about waking him up in the morning. A clear statement of the problem will make problem solving easier.

In stating both opinions be sure to give each side its just due. For example, your saying, "I don't want you going to the show alone because I am concerned about your safety" may be reasonable but if you then describe your child's position by saying, "and you don't care about safety," or, "and you resent me telling you what to do," that's not fair. Describe your child's feelings as you would in reflecting; for example, "and you feel you are old enough to go on your own without supervision."

The more precisely you define the disagreement, the easier it will be to propose compromises. If you are concerned about safety try to identify exactly when the fear is aroused. Are you concerned about your child getting to the show, during show time, or after the show lets out? If your worry is the time period when the show lets out, then concentrate on that time span rather than the entire evening.

See if your child poses solutions to the disagreement and encourage his involvement. When he offers outrageous solutions respond by ignoring them or offering equally outrageous solutions. This is a learning situation that forces your child into offering creative ideas which "fit", that is, solutions which both sides will agree to. At first, you will offer most of the solutions in a priming-the-pump fashion. Quickly move to a position where your child takes over this burden. As he takes on more of the responsibility for problem solving you should resist offering your (good) solutions. Let him struggle. Teaching him to struggle for answers is more valuable in the long run than the immediate solution.

The major element in the negotiation process is compromise. Neither side may get everything they want but the most important points are satisfied. Mother may not be completely satisfied with daughter going to the show alone but feels comfortable enough to let her go when mother's principal worry of daughter coming home when it is dark is solved when daughter persuades her older brother to drive her home after the show. Parents may decide to accept the compromise of a later bed time if son is in his room and quiet. The extra time he gets to stay up will not disturb the parents' peace. The solution of giving the boy an alarm clock may also reduce your burden of waking him in the morning.

When the compromise is reached be sure to clearly state the terms and have your child agree to them. The reason to summarize the negotiated points is to check that both sides understand the obligations and terms of the agreement. This last step will help to avoid misunderstandings that arise later on. It might be a good idea to write the compromise as if it were a contract, having both sides sign the document.

Give the plan a try. State how the compromise is working. This will either serve to reward your child for helping solve a problem or will serve to begin modifying the bargain if it didn't work well. Modify the compromise using the same negotiation process, focusing on what now needs a change.

Throughout the entire process of negotiating you are assuming a partnership role. The more successful you are at dropping the parental (and sometimes authoritarian) role the freer you can be in adopting a partnership role.

CHAPTER 3
APPLYING THE TECHNIQUES TO REACH OUR GOALS

Child Rearing: What To Do Now

This chapter is where we put it all together — the techniques and goals. Here is a practical way to accomplish the broad goals described earlier. It is not exactly a cookbook since there are endless variations and combinations which will serve your purpose. This section is more of a guide in assisting you to select and use the techniques in the most effective ways.

In my years of counseling I have listened to how parents select various techniques to accomplish hoped-for goals. Parents have reasonable intentions and often have a logical explanation for the plan they chose. Only, the plan often didn't work. While it sounded reasonable the technique backfired. Let me give you several examples of how reasonable-sounding practices led to failure:

Jim left his bicycle out all night again. His parents wanted to teach him a lesson so they took the bicycle away from Jim for two weeks. The parents reasoned that the punishment would teach the boy to remember to take the bike in at night.

Mary spends her money "foolishly". Her parents decide on a plan to teach her to spend money more wisely. They decide to give her money only if Mary gives them a "good" reason. In this way the parents hope that Mary will learn that she can have money for useful purposes, but not for foolish things.

Marty is a bully. His parents decide that they need to break him of the habit of beating up younger kids. The parents decide to administer harsh corporal punishment when they learn that Marty has assaulted a younger child. They believe that in this way Marty will learn what it is like to pick on people younger than himself.

Tom does not take good care of his dog (i.e., feeding, keeping clean, and putting it out at night). His parents threaten that if Tom doesn't start doing a better job they will sell the dog. Tom doesn't improve and the dog is given away. The parents believe that this procedure teaches children to be more responsible.

The above examples all backfired. Perhaps you can guess why. Jim wasn't in the *habit* of being responsible with his bike. Taking the bike away for such a long time did not help Jim *practice* the habit of bringing it in at night. It actually led Jim into forgetting about the bike, just the opposite of what his parents believed would happen. When Jim did get the bike back he promptly left it out again. This time his frustrated parents scolded him, which didn't make any more of an impression than when the bike was taken away.

Mary similarly didn't learn how to spend money "responsibly" as her parents had hoped. Whatever money she did manage to obtain continued to be spent on candy and ice cream. Mary did learn, however, to find ways of deceiving her parents. Thus, she was able to maintain her "irresponsible" habit by lying.

Marty didn't learn to be more peaceful. He was soon placed in foster care. When that didn't work he was institutionalized because of his assaultive behavior. His parents say he was born that way.

Tom resented his parents for giving away "his" dog. Tom's experience was similar to Jim's. Neither boy learned the *habit* of doing a chore. Rather than repeat the habit daily the result was that the chore, taking the bike in at night, was removed. Learning didn't take place.

With the examples given, the selection and application of a technique was not appropriate. Why? For Jim and Tom the technique of consequences was used. The technique was not appropriate because either the consequence was a one-time event or was not frequent enough to do the teaching. A better guide would have been to employ the technique of rules, with stress on repetition. Yes, there would be a consequence, but that consequence could be repeated daily so that a habit develops.

Mary was given so little freedom; there was no penalty for spending (as the parents put it) "foolishly". There would always be more money for the nonfoolish items. The horn of plenty was always full. Her only task was to divert as much money into candy as possible. The technique of consequences was not applied appropriately. If Mary was on a more limited budget (possibly set through negotiation) she would have to choose between the candy and other items she wanted. The consequence would be in missing out on desired things if she chose to buy candy. While there is no guarantee Mary would (always) forgo the candy, I believe she would begin to learn better budgeting — which her parents really wanted to teach.

Finally, Marty's parents were not aware of the power of modeling. Rather than learn by the imposed (trial-and-error) punishment for bully behavior, Marty learned through his parents modeling assaultive behavior. Marty's father was later arrested for wife beating.

I want to now examine each of the broad goals mentioned earlier, Being Responsible, Feeling Good About Oneself, Likable, and Communicates Well, and provide you with tips on how to approach each goal.

Being Responsible

Being responsible means a person does what is expected without being continually reminded. The transformation from a rather irresponsible, self-centered infant to a responsible young adult is miraculous. Yet that miracle doesn't happen automatically nor is it inherited. Your child will learn to be responsible primarily through your guidance and teaching. Here are some policies which help you in your task:

1. *Don't take over your child's responsibility.* Perhaps one of the easiest ways of teaching a child to be responsible is to allow them to be responsible for themselves. A good example of what this means is when children make a mess. Regardless of whether the mess was deliberate, such as leaving toys and clothing strewn about, or unintentional due to an accident, the issue is, who cleans up the mess? Parents may punish or excuse the mess but there remains the task of clean-up. The value you want to teach is being responsible and therefore your policy should be to consistently have the child clean up these

messes. If the child is too young to accomplish the entire clean-up then have him contribute some part in the clean-up process, however small and meaningless it appears.

With respect to the Ten Techniques examined in Chapter 2 the method suggested here is the technique of "Consequences", not the one on "Modeling". It is more effective for the child to struggle with the consequences of his actions than to watch you clean up afterward.

Other examples of taking responsibility upon yourself include situations where it's your child's responsibility to plan ahead. There are times when a child wants money, transportation, or an alibi because he failed to plan ahead. Teaching responsibility means that he goes without or suffers the consequences for not meeting obligations in advance.

As a parent you don't want to deprive your child of fun. Nevertheless, by bailing him out of a bind you may be robbing him of the opportunity to learn responsibility. Paying the price is a powerful lesson which people need to learn. It's probably best that they learn early when the consequences are less damaging. You're not being cruel when you stand by and watch your child suffer the consequences of his actions. You're teaching him that people usually reap what they sow.

Other techniques you may want to consider are: Reflective Listening, Saving Face and Trial-and-Error Learning. By using reflective listening it keeps you from interfering in your child's responsibility. It is his burden to arrive at a solution. By avoiding the implication that, "if you only did what I told you to do then this wouldn't have happened", it allows face saving relief to the already frustrated child. Stepping back and allowing trial-and-error learning to take place keeps you from taking on your child's responsibility.

2. *Give your child something to be responsible for.* I am a strong advocate of giving children chores to do. By using the technique of Rules you can begin giving even very young children an obligation to perform. Whether the chore is picking up toys, cleaning up after themselves, or some other daily chore the idea of having your children contribute regularly to your family is a good one. Pick long-term chores, only a few of them and don't be afraid to rigidly enforce a long-standing chore rule.

3. *Responsibility is a habit.* Children are not born with it and may not learn it "naturally". Infants are rather selfish creatures and we accept the selfishness as a matter of course. Being socially responsible is a matter of learning. The process is gradual. Starting with tangible *external* consequences, your child will learn over years of repetition to make the rewards *internal.* Don't expect him to automatically want to contribute his share by carrying out the trash or feeding the dog. Children don't feel obliged to work just because their parents support them. Learning through repetition is the key. Habits are based upon repetition. Repeating chores over the years makes the chore seem to the child that it is his responsibility rather than a chore given him. Your child will take *ownership* of routine responsibilities only after much repetition. Responsibility is a habit.

4. *Develop a good sense of property rights.* Taking care of one's own and other people's property is important in our culture. Philosophically, some of us may not like the intense strivings for possession in our western culture. Ideally, it may be more civilized and spiritually

lifting to see property as ownerless. "What's mine is everyone's and what's everyone's I may use according to my need." Fine and dandy but that's not here and now; it's not the world in which your children will live. So if you want your children to take care of their belongings and be respectful of other's property you will need to incorporate this goal in your plan. Make some things your exclusive property. If your child wants to use those specific things have him ask permission. Don't be afraid to say, "No, you can't use it now." Likewise, allow your child to own something, with you asking his permission to use it. This way he will learn the responsibility of owning and borrowing.

By having your children earn an allowance they learn the need for work and the value of money. That may sound pristine; nevertheless, it's true. Children will learn to save for those things they desire. Don't always come through when Johnny or Mary wants his or her "big" thing. Experiencing *controlled* disappointments at an early age makes it easier to overcome future disappointments — even to avoid some. Automatically replacing broken toys is also a poor habit to form. Let your child know the pain of losing something mishandled. He will learn a healthier respect for his possessions.

After reading the above four policies you may start to feel that childhood is a chamber of horrors. So far our poor child has had to endure pain and frustration at each turn. Actually, life normally brings many setbacks. What is highlighted is allowing nature to teach many lessons without parents needlessly interfering. In a positive way, you can then be freed of many burdens, while taking the role of a caring and sympathetic listener.

5. Using the *"Ten Techniques."* Below are listed the

Ten Techniques with brief notes on how to apply each to the goal of Being Responsible:

Modeling. Make sure you are living as responsible a life as you want your children to live.

Trial-and-error. This technique is good for "learning the hard way". The trial-and-error method of learning allows outside forces (social or physical) to do the teaching rather than you.

Rules. This is an excellent technique for teaching habits and chores. Rules are good for repetitive tasks.

Ignoring is not a particularly useful or applicable tool for teaching responsibility (unless you want to consider ignoring your child's gripes and bellyaches).

Consequences. This is an excellent tool for demonstrating responsibility. There is a consequence for acceptable or unacceptable behavior. Try to rely on rules for the repetitive situations and consequences for the occasional situations. One basic difference between the two techniques is that rules are pre-established routines while consequences imply a judgement that you impose on your child as a result of a rather new behavior. Consequences are more of a spontaneous decision which follows an approved or disapproved action. One of the best forms of consequences to use is, "Go back and do it again 'til it is correct." Another good use is to clean up, replace, or repair whatever the mess or damage.

Love. This non-contingent reward is not specifically of value in teaching responsibility.

Humor lessens the burdens of responsibility. There is no reason why you can't make chores or tasks more fun by adding laughter and humor to the situation. The more pleasant and light-hearted you can be, the better.

52

Reflective listening. A fine way of not assuming responsibility of your kids is to reflect their feelings. The "problem" is for your child to solve; struggling to solve a reasonable problem is part of being responsible. Don't spend time reflecting feelings when your child should be doing something which she hasn't done yet. Have her do the task then listen to her feelings.

Saving face. Being responsible is sometimes difficult enough without your adding humiliation, lectures, and I-told-you-so's. Don't say, "If you'd have only listened to me you wouldn't have had all that extra work." If your child learns through trial-and-error or consequences then allow her to save face if something goes wrong. Sometimes, if a word is worth a dollar, silence is worth two. Silence can allow face-saving. A word of support or a reflected feeling is also a good face-saving device.

Negotiation. Use negotiation in setting rules. Negotiation is also helpful in identifying who has responsibility and for what. The very process of negotiation demonstrates a certain level of responsibility in your child.

In review, a list of strategies to help children learn to be responsible include:

Don't take over your child's responsibility.

Give your child something to be responsible for.

Responsibility is a habit.

Develop a good sense of property rights.

Use the "Ten Techniques".

Feeling Good About Oneself

Recalling that this general goal was composed of such desirable traits as being confident, independent, assertive, sticking up for one's self, not relying on chemical crutches, and having self-esteem; how might you work toward meeting this broad goal?

Philosophically there is a major difference in understanding the process of "feeling good". Our Western culture has generally viewed the process as the result of accomplishment. You feel good when you are productive and come close to meeting your expectations. Through actions and strivings you evaluate yourself. On the other hand, an Eastern philosophy would describe feeling good about oneself as an inner peace, a tranquility. Emphasis is less on actions, sometimes on the absence of actions. So, does feeling good come from within or is it acquired through actions? This question is one of the many reasons why teaching your child to feel good about himself is difficult.

Another difficulty comes in the form of balance. While it is desirable to possess some confidence, independence, and self-esteem, an overabundance has negative qualities (e.g., "know-it-all", loner, stuck up, egotistical, etc.).

Feeling good about yourself seems quite beyond the capacity of an infant. An infant has no pride, dignity, respect or humility. It's about as dependent and helpless as Santa Claus without a chimney. An infant may be assertive when crying, but doesn't have the ability to do much about the injustice of not being fed on time or staying in wet diapers.

We know from experiments on infant monkeys and, to some extend, on human infants that having a soft, warm mother (or mother substitute) to touch is essential for healthy development. Therefore, you need to provide your infant with frequent physical contact. Fortunately, you are likely to provide the needed contact, naturally, without special training. Your infant develops a sense of security through repeated physical contact. How much contact is enough and can there be too much physical contact are questions which are presently unanswerable.

Another line of investigation about infants has focused on what has been called "bonding". Bonding is a strong attachment between you and your infant. Some investigations suggest that the bond may begin in the first hours after birth. By seeing and touching your baby in the first hour and frequently thereafter, a much stronger attachment is made than if the infant were isolated from you. Touching, caressing, rocking, patting, and speaking to your newborn, are the actions which help to provide a close bond. What happens if a bond is not made between parent and infant? We don't exactly know but some experts believe that the infant will suffer problems in forming close relationships with people throughout the child's life. I am confident that we will hear much about bonding and early childhood development in the future. Already, we know that some forms of mental retardation can be cured from intensive changes early in the child's life. Further ideas on these early childhood years are discussed in the chapter entitled "Developmental Timetable".

Feeling good about oneself is vitally important to our sense of well being. A low opinion of ourselves can be accompanied by jealousy, fear of rejection, and insecurity. We expect, yet fear, criticism. While it is clear that positive feelings about yourself are indispensable for sustained happiness, exactly how it is developed is rather

mysterious. Five general sources are discussed below which intuitively appear to contribute to one's self-worth:
1. *Parental contribution.* Parents who provide a stable, non-judgemental home, offer greater security to kids. The technique of non-contingent Love is of immense value. Knowing that your parents accept you with all your frailties provides an excellent foundation. It follows that others will accept you even if they know all your weaknesses and faults.

The technique of Consequences includes sharing with your children how you feel about their behavior. Often knowing how others (parents) feel, gets rid of doubts and misconceptions. It's a good practice to tell (not yell at) children when they make you upset, infuriate you, or disappoint you. If that's how you feel it is better to say it openly. Children and adults have more bad feelings about themselves when they don't know how others are feeling.

You may wonder how, on one hand, you provide a non-judgemental home (non-contingent love) while at the same time making what appears to be negative judgements (consequences) about the child's behavior. The differences lie in the way you state your negative feelings. You are making a statement about how you feel, a statement about your emotional state. By saying you are sad, angry, disappointed, desperate, or frustrated you are describing how you feel when you see a particular behavior. Basically you are telling your child how the *behavior* makes you feel. This is still a non-judgemental position because you are not judging the child, only the behavior. If you were to say things such as:

you're stupid	why are you so shy?
what's wrong with you?	you're a cry baby

you're selfish
you're lazy

grow up!
you never finish any-
thing

why are you always so
backward?

in response to your child's behavior then it would be judgemental! Rather than share your internal feelings you would be making a critical judgement about your child. These repetitive, critical statements can and often do stick with children throughout their lifetime. It undermines self-worth. It is extraordinarily difficult to overcome such a label even though intellectually we may know that the criticism is ridiculous. You want to convey the feeling that you accept and value your child without reservation. You may disapprove of some behaviors, but you value your child regardless. You can express your criticisms more constructively by using examples such as the following:

When you make a mistake such as that I get frustrated and impatient. (Not, "you're stupid.")

Sometimes, when you won't let your younger sister play with your toys, I'm very disappointed. I feel that it is important to share with those close to you. (Not, "you're selfish.")

When I see you sitting in front of the TV while I'm working I get jealous and irritated. I'm jealous because I can't be relaxing and enjoying myself and irritated because I may wind up having to do extra work. (Not, "you're lazy".)

When you don't get your way it hurts, but, when you cry that way I get angry because I think you're trying to get sympathy and manipulate me. (Not, "you're a cry baby.")

When I see you leave things unfinished I get furious. I'm furious because I've always felt it was important for me to finish what I set out to do. (Not, "you never finish anything.")

The above samples give you more constructive ways to express your criticism.

2. *Life style contribution.* Being able to routinely accomplish chores and tasks makes us feel good about ourselves. We judge ourself by our accomplishments. If your child is expected to regularly finish certain chores it establishes a life pattern. The pattern is one of positive accomplishment.

An opposite life style, one of being lazy and procrastinating, highlights the need for adopting an energetic routine. It may sound like I'm pushing the work ethic: happiness through work. Well, I am a bit. There are people who rather effectively argue that until we rid ourselves of measuring people by their actions, we will always be burdened by our fallibility. We can never do enough and therefore we can never completely feel content with ourselves. The reader is free to make his/her own decision here.

The line of logic for suggesting forming a habit of accomplishment is that for most of us, reaching the end of a list of chores or even finishing the first item on the list makes us feel good. We see ourselves and others see us as energetic, industrious and healthy. Encouraging such a life style, I believe, should be part of your child-rearing policy. Giving children a gradually increasing number of useful chores helps the pattern to develop. Children who routinely complete work feel good about the accomplishments and themselves. Review the techniques of Rules and Consequences to implement such a policy.

3. *Dedication.* This element is somewhat similar to the life style contribution in that it also highlights self-satisfaction through actions. Dedication here means persistence at a task. Dedication is having a goal that you pursue despite frustration. Setting a goal that is pursued over periods of days or years helps give your child confidence and a sense of well being. Learning to be persistent in the face of immediate failure may turn that treat of failure into a success.

Exactly how you teach your child to be persistent is not completely clear. By using the technique of Consequences you can encourage "stick with it" activity. A well placed remark can serve to have a child maintain interest in something. Providing incentives for continuing school studies also helps. For example, taking your child to see some aspect of what he is studying (in a museum, on a trip, out in the country, to a zoo, or library) is a good idea. Certainly this is a delicate effort because if you thrust your enthusiasm upon him there is a tendency for him to back off.

Another aspect of dedication is the finishing of a project. Children should be encouraged to complete (within reason) whatever they undertake. I am disturbed by what I see is a growing trend to always give credit for *"some"* effort, without stressing the *completion* of the task. I am totally in favor of beginning training with rewarding or acknowledging behavior in the desired direction. What bothers me is that often there is no follow through. A child can satisfy a requirement only by showing some effort. He is not held accountable for completing the task. This practice is plentiful in schools throughout the country. Children are passed along as a result of a set of incomplete efforts. This same policy is prevalent within the home. If a child completes part of what is wanted, parents begin to feel sorry for or impatient with the child and finish the burden themselves. I hear parents say that they can't stand to listen to Bobbie's grumbling about some chore. After a short time Bobbie is sent away and mother completes the job.

When does persistence at a task become ridiculous? Sometimes a child picks an impossible task only to get hopelessly bogged down at the start. Let your child struggle a reasonable while before coming to his rescue. It will take many, many such experiences before he learns to measure the task accurately. Taking an accurate measure of a task is an important skill to learn. It also may be that with a little of your help, a bottleneck will be overcome and your child can continue in the task. Trial-and-error experiences and Reflective Listening techniques can be helpful when trying to encourage dedication.

4. *Peer contact.* Not all of a child's self-worth comes from your parental influence. Some (but we don't know how much) comes from a child's interaction with peers. Even here you can exert considerable force. You can help determine your children's friends by providing easy access to more "acceptable" friends. Families can spend time with the families of preferred playmates or can transport children to the homes of more acceptable children. I expect that this form of screening can be overdone. On the other hand, you are partially products of your interactions with others. Being around more trouble-free children is healthier than a constant dose of problem chil-

dren. This screening and encouraging function is best done informally, without lectures, and while the child is young. By the pre-teen years you will find channeling more difficult.

It's a frustrating and useless task to argue with your child about his or her friends. Your child probably knows very well whom you find acceptable or unacceptable. The problem I see is not that a peer is likely to adversely influence your child (although that can certainly happen), but that your child shares something with his friends. We are usually like our friends in many ways. So, if your child hangs around with unacceptable or troubled kids, your child probably also shares the friends' unacceptable or troubled behavior. The answer would be to change the undesirable behavior pattern. Hopefully, you will see a change in friends.

The techniques of Rules, Reflecting, and Love are important techniques to use here.

5. *The unexpected.* New and strange situations are constantly arising in most people's lives. If your child has had many chances to make decisions about an unexpected event, he is less likely to be shaken by another new demand. What happens to children sheltered from new and different encounters? The answer probably is later on he will be unsure of himself, apprehensive about life, afraid to struggle with a new development and will shy away from change. Here again the parent wants to take a non-intervention posture, if possible. Allow the child to meet and struggle with the unexpected. This builds confidence and optimism about the future.

Summing up the various contributing factors influencing a child's ability to feel good about himself we have

the following:
Parental contribution   Peer contact
Life style contribution   The unexpected
Dedication

Likable
Some of the specific goals which contribute to developing a likable person include: pleasantness, warmth, agreeability, humility, caring, generosity, respect for others, willingness to make compromises, and a sense of humor. We enjoy having others enjoy us and especially want others to like our children. As one mother put it, having a likeable child, "makes me feel all warm and fuzzy inside."

There is a broad and complex set of individual goals that contribute to being liked. Below are some contributing factors to the general goal with specific techniques to help arrive at this goal.

1. *Being positive.* I know several people who have the singular disposition of being positive. Perhaps they recognize the negative features surrounding life, but they either manage to avoid the negative or they selectively pick that little glimmer of goodness from the bleak background. It is nearly impossible to dislike them; in fact, I am compelled to like them. Being positive is catching. When I am around positive people I feel healthier and happier. Positive people are more likable.

I also have friends whom I doubt have voiced a positive comment in years. Beginning with an angry birth cry they can't help but find a little glimmer of badness in an almost perfect object or action. Being negative is catching. When I am around negative people it is easier to be more critical and judgmental. I walk away from an encounter with unhappy and depressed people feeling drained and unhappy.

In contrasting my positive friends from the negativistic ones I believe that both groups are living a life of regularity and respectability. Each have consistent life styles. It was probably no easier for one group to be the way they are than the other the opposite. Being positive or negative is a life-long habit. If the habit leans toward being a generally positive individual, life will be more pleasant and people will find you more likable. If the habit is negative then the quality of life is markedly reduced and people will avoid you.

The above may sound elementary and naive, but I am impressed at the impact predisposed habits have on the quality of life lived. How can you begin assuring your child a more positive, and consequently likable, nature? In the list of techniques, Modeling usually tops the list as a tool for accomplishing what is desired. If you want your child to be likable, you ought to be a positive individual. This task, for some an unbelievably difficult undertaking, means that the daily frequency of positive to negative comments must shift in the desired direction. Perhaps, simply adding additional positive comments will suffice or you may need to actually reduce the negative comments.

A technique which has enthusiastic adherents is to count thoughts or behaviors that are desired or undesired. For example, you could choose to literally count (with a golf counter-type device or with paper and pencil) the number of positive statements made per day. A record is kept and even charted to see progress toward the goal of increased positive comments. Another tact might be to count negative comments with the goal of reducing that count. Conceivably, you might keep a record of both positive and negative statements.

The counting technique is an excellent one which demands persistence. When I used this simple technique on myself I found out that counting (I used an inexpensive golf-type counter because it was easier to remember to wear on my wrist than carrying paper and pencil in my shirt pocket) did facilitate my awareness of the subject I was targeting. Within a short period, one week, I saw a marked change in my behavior. I also found that prematurely stopping the counting procedure tends to wash most of the desired progress away. As with any attempt at changing behavior, the change must be continued for long periods of time in order for the new behavior to become a habit. The counting procedure is tedious, but it accomplishes the goal. Remember, the goal is to have you, the parent, become more positive, thereby serving as a good model for your children.

One aspect to being positive is being complimentary. Delivering a genuine compliment to someone is like biblically casting bread upon the water. Giving a compliment starts a chain reaction; it can even rebound back to you. Get into the habit of giving compliments. Give them to people when your child is present and give them to your child. For those of you who have trouble complimenting my advice is, force yourself! The initial compliments you give will be uncomfortable, awkward, and unimpressive to you. Don't worry. The recipient of your compliment probably won't know the difference. He/she will be delighted to get the compliment and won't notice its faults as much as you do.

Incidentally, if you're not used to complimenting, you may also not be comfortable accepting compliments. Actually, many people have difficulty accepting compliments with grace. You may not receive compliments frequently enough to practice receiving compliments. Nevertheless, since you already cast out the first small pieces of bread you should expect to receive a compliment back sooner or later. You should learn how to accept a compliment graciously. Again, this may seem awkward at first if you usually reject compliments; but remember, the giver of the compliment may be more concerned with his task of giving you the compliment than in your "forced" receipt of it.

A good reply to a compliment is, "Thanks, I really appreciate your saying that," or, "Gee, it makes me feel good that you feel that way." At the very least, give a hearty, "Thank you!", although I recommend more. What you have done by graciously acknowledging the compliment is reward the complimenter. The complimenter is likely to give more compliments in the future. In all, a very positive state of affairs.

The technique of Humor belongs in a discussion of how to have children become likable. An armchair observation is that people who are positive are more humorous and laugh more than people more predominantly negative. The technique of Humor involves smiling, laughing at oneself, and laughing non-critically at others. A laugh a day, whether a big belly jiggle or a more sedate smile would go a long way to ensure your child a lighter and more enjoyable life, not to mention the benefits you will derive from this exercise.

We have been examining ways you can model behavior which will help your children toward the goal of being more likable. If you are like myself, you will find it difficult to change your behavior even though you know it will effect good changes or establish a good pattern in your children. Changing yourself so that your children will pick up the good habits is the best way I know of to meet the goal. It works! Your children will easily adopt the desired behavior once you have.

2. *Being generous.* A component of being likable is being generous. Being generous is quite contrary to an infant's nature and strains many adults. In order to teach generosity, the procedure begins with sharing. Begin modeling the sharing behavior at an early age. This can be accomplished by sharing something, food or playthings, with the toddler. Say something such as, "Mommy is going to share her peaches with Johnnie." Periodically, the parent puts food on Johnnie's plate and says, "Does Johnnie want to share his fruit with mommy?" Try to start by putting a clear excess amount of fruit in Johnnie's bowl so that sharing does not equate with losing. This procedure can be effectively managed when you have one item and the child another. By sharing, Johnnie learns that he will receive something in return.

The sharing procedure means that your child owns or possesses the object(s). At first, the toddler may choose *not* to share. It then becomes reasonable for mommy to say in response to her stingy tike, "Mommy is unhappy that Johnnie is not sharing." That type of statement can be followed by mother's quick exit, thereby emphasizing the point. Gradually, through repetition, Johnnie learns to share. As he grows older, Johnnie learns that sharing doesn't necessarily result in an immediate exchange. The return becomes an, "I appreciate that," or a "Thank you." Sharing then becomes the act of being generous. Being generous doesn't mean carelessly giving without regard, a capacity we more aptly describe as foolish. Consequently, even with generosity, there is the expectation that we will receive some return. Perhaps there is no tangible return or a tit-for-tat return nor even an immediate return, but we expect some return. Your child naturally learns the meaning of this when he shares with other youngsters and occasionally does not receive any return from a particular child. Your child learns through the technique of Consequences to be somewhat discriminating with his generosity. Don't interfere with the minor injustices your child receives from other children. Keep in mind that he is learning a valuable lesson early, which will help him through his later life.

I hear parents complain that their children do not share. In order to genuinely share, a child should first "own" something. I have asked children to make up lists of things they own, things that others must ask permission before using. When a child begins to feel that he owns something without the parental threat of losing it, he can see it is to his advantage to share. He gets permission to use someone's things in exchange. Children will naturally develop sharing with playmates if there is no parental interference. By interference I mean threats, lectures, or actions which insist on sharing or cooperating.

There are lots of toys and games on the market which stress sharing. Most games have at least the taking turns aspect. Pick out games which promote cooperation rather than always selecting competitive games.

We have been examining sharing as a first step toward achieving the generosity goal. Our culture holds an ambivalent attitude toward generosity. On one hand we see material possessions as highly important. On the other hand we value the act of giving up those valuable possessions to others. There is a complex learning task here: value possessions yet value people over possessions. It is even more complex when taking into account who is worthy of your generosity and to what extent.

3. *Showing warmth.* People who show concern for our well being are naturally more likable. If we "know" that a particular person has our best interest at heart we relax our defenses. One of the best ways to show concern is by using the technique of Reflective Listening. Parents show concern by listening patiently and throughly. Then, after listening, you let her know you paid attention to her by reflecting back her words and feelings.

In order to insert warmth you need to go beyond mere reflecting. You need to state your child's thoughts in a way she finds acceptable. As a counselor, I frequently use reflective listening. I may say to a pair of struggling parents, "You really want to do the right thing: you're concerned about your child's well being," or, "The reason you decided upon that particular disciplinary plan was that you sincerely hoped it would help your child." Thus, by reflecting to the parents that I understand the positive motivation behind their actions, some of the parents defenses are eased. I am showing compassion for the parents' *intent.* Hopefully, I will be better liked and seen as being warmer because the parents feel that I understand the intent of their action.

In order to teach children to show warmth, you must

first model the behavior. Therefore, you model reflective listening. Try to capture the positive intent in your child's words or actions. Examples of such reflecting are: "I know you really didn't intend to break that vase. It was an accident." "You would like to do better on your school work, but other things interfere." "You didn't purposely set out to get into a fight; you just couldn't avoid it." Generally, I find most people do not actively intend to do "harm" to others. The harm comes through mistakes, negligence, misunderstandings, omission, confusion, lack of preparation, or by accident. Harm usually is an unintentional byproduct. Rather than assuming the other party was deliberatley harmful or knew full well their actions would bring unpleasantness, we would usually be more accurate to assume it an error. By reflecting the positive intent of the act and minimizing the accidental harm, we show compassion.

My generalization of harm being accidental is almost universal in children. Even their deliberately harmful acts can often be seen as inept attempts at reaching some positive goal such as friendship or attention. I have found only a very few examples of children being deliberately "bad". A child may seem deliberately bad when he is spontaneously responding to being hurt. A child may strike out, due to his own pain, and "deliberately" destroy something. I stress the spontaneity of such a reflex. You can clearly see the harmful act almost immediately following the child's pain. Children do not tend to have the capacity (or inclination) to scheme and get even by preparing an elaborate counter attack. They are not that patient and diabolical. When a child strikes out it is because he hurts so much that he doesn't know what else to

69

do. Your reflecting that he didn't actually plan his destructiveness but did it out of pain, models warmth and understanding. Your child will gradually (spontaneously) respond to your modeling by showing concern and warmth back.

There may be the extraordinarily rare occurrence of a deliberately malevolent child. This type of child would be severely (emotionally) disturbed and can quickly be recognized as "different". These instances are so rare that I personally have never seen a young child which I would accept as being chronically and naturally malevolent or bad.

Showing warmth is accomplished by non-verbal behavior. A kind smile, touch, nod, wink, and good eye contact reflect concern. Perhaps the most significant means of conveying warmth is how you appear rather than exactly what you say. Warmth is conveyed by a mellow tone in the voice, by a non-threatening movement toward the person, and by accepting movements or gestures. The eyes are frequently recognized as conveying the most amount of non-verbal information. Narrowing the space between the eyelids or wrinkling the eyebrows doesn't show the warmth as fully opened eyes. If you don't know how your facial expressions are interpreted by others, ask some close friends. There will probably be a great degree of agreement between your friends on how they interpret your facial gestures or body movements. Modeling warmth and acceptance is the key in having children learn how to show warmth.

The technique of Humor can effectively teach your child to show warmth. Principally, the parent models the technique of Humor by making fun of some situation.

Humor is appropriate when it makes fun in such a way as to be non-threatening and non-critical. By laughing at yourself it conveys an acceptance of another's failures or frailties. The technique might take the form of, "If you think that was bad, listen to this: _____." Don't overuse that form, though. If the recipient doesn't "get the joke" or doesn't feel comfortable with your humor then discontinue it. Humor is only a good technique when accepted by the recipient.

4. *Showing respect.* People are seen as more likeable when they show respect for those around them. Teaching children to be respectful of others, of people and property, is accomplished through a variety of techniques: modeling, negotiating, reflecting without taking action, consequences, and ignoring.

Model showing respect for your child's property by asking his permission to use "his" things. When possible, allow the child time to finish whatever he is doing before helping you. Avoid being sarcastic or autocratic. Don't talk down to children — they are extraordinarily sensitive to being talked down to.

The technique of Negotiating communicates parental respect; it also teaches children that they can profit by showing you respect. In negotiations both sides must feel good about the solution. Your child gradually learns that by recognizing your needs and satisfying most of them you will react favorably to his needs.

Reflecting children's feelings without telling them what to do or without solving their problems demonstrates respect for their problem-solving ability. You are respecting the child's views and opinions, thereby modeling what you want your child to do.

71

The technique of Consequences can be employed in order to demosntrate the need to respect property. If your child negligently broke a toy don't simply replace the toy with a new one or a substitute. The pain of lost or broken toys will naturally teach care (respect) for possessions. You can let your child know that you recognize his pain by saying: "I know you miss that toy; you want mother to buy you another one;" or, "I bet you're angry at someone taking it." While you can empathize, don't run to the rescue.

If your child doesn't seem bothered by his losing or destroying his possession, you (or relatives) may be showering him with too many presents. The solution to too many possessions which leads to carelessness is easy — stop giving. Withhold gifts from relatives, if necessary. Let your child suffer the consequence of going without for a while. Then gradually give the toys, but don't overdo it again.

Ignoring can be effective when children are arguing, fighting, or squabbling. Ignoring sibling conflicts allows children the opportunity to work out their own compromises. Siblings learn by trial-and-error how to get along. They learn how to show respect for sibling property *without* parental intervention.

Showing respect for children calls for interpreting what they say — in the correct light. Frequently, parents listen to children only long enough to twist the child's words to prove him wrong or prove the parent right. Showing respect means reflecting your child's words in such a light as to make what he says "logical". In effect, do not hold your child to his exact words. Try to capture the meaning and thought behind the words. By showing understanding you show respect. Modeling the policy of putting your child's words into an understandable light will be repeated by your child.

A final way to model respect is to be tolerant of the child's opinions. By listening patiently when your child has an opinion other than yours, you demonstrate respect. By gently saing, "I can see you feel strongly about that," or after reflecting accurately what your child said, say, "I see it differently than you do." Challenging your children can thus be accomplished in a respectful fashion. You can certainly disagree if you do it with gentleness and dignity. In time your child will respond by showing you more respect for your parental views.

5. *Agreeable.* Having the quality of being agreeable makes your child a pleasure to be around. Being agreeable means to pick out the areas you agree with or see merit in and voice your approval. "That's a good idea," is a way of focusing on the positive side. Being agreeable does not mean being a constant "yes man" or a mindless tag along. It means that you maximize your areas of agreement while still maintaining areas of disagreement. By stressing what you agree with, your child will emphasize those points. In a sense, it will bring a greater payoff to the child to pursue the areas of agreement. There won't be as much payoff in areas which you ignore or gently disagree with.

If you don't like something what can you do? Sure, you can directly state your opposition. You can also indirectly respond to the issue by voicing a positive comment about an alternative. My point here is to urge you to minimize your skepticism, reservations, pessimism, caution, and opposition. It's too easy to be negative toward your child's ideas. Being more positive and encouraging seems to take more thought.

By using the technique of Negotiating, your child will learn to identify the areas of compromise and agreement. The more areas of agreement, the more likely your child will "get" part of what he wants.

An important dimension to being likable is the ability to accept some degree of defeat, gracefully. Accepting less than what you hoped for, with grace and tact, is a key to being "easy going" and likable. Modeling is the most appropriate technique to teach this quality. Overdoing this quality is labeled as being a "pollyanna." I don't think it would hurt for most of us to move closer to being a pollyanna, particularly toward children.

We have been examining ways in which being likable can be taught to your children. The techniques that have been particularly stressed were modeling and reflective listening. Children will learn to be likable if it pays off, if they are rewarded for being likable. Fortunately, people reward others with attention and material things when they like someone. Therefore, a parent is priming the pump by modeling likable behavior. Once the child imitates what he sees then the trial-and-error principal will lead him into more likable behavior. Being likable is a pattern of behavior. It becomes a habit early in life and usually is maintained throughout life.

Summarizing the issue and elements contributing to a policy of teaching likableness we find the following:

Being positive	Showing respect
Being generous	Agreeable
Showing warmth	

By using the above five ideas you will find it much easier to encourage likableness in your child.

Communicates Well

The fourth and final major goal is to teach children how to communicate with others. We all communicate, but few of us feel as though we have mastered this two-phase skill. One phase is getting our ideas across; the other is accurately receiving the ideas of others.

1. *Language development.* Researchers are discovering that children who use language well tended to have parents (particularly mothers) who talked more to the infant. Beginning at birth, it is important that your child be exposed to language. Talk to your child frequently. "Now I am going to change your diaper. Let's go to the nursery and you can lie down." It doesn't matter what you say. Just talk!

The next major phase is when your child begins learning words. Most parents *do* spend time repeating words and articulating sounds. That's excellent. Because of your enthusiasm your toddler will continue struggling with words. Gradually the toddler learns that he can effect a change in the environment through language. Having a child capture your attention with language is instrumental in good development. Carefully reward your youngster's advances in language with your attention and enthusiasm.

Let your child struggle with words, particularly if he becomes "lazy." Some children get sidetracked when their needs are met through immature vocalizations. Try to insist upon increasingly more sophistication in your child's language *before* complying with his demands. You can accomplish this by saying, "I don't understand; what do you want?" If your child persists in immature use of

75

language you should ignore his requests when you know he is not trying hard enough. This definitely should be the policy when your child has already clearly articulated his request in the past.

2. *Transmitting a message.* In order to help your child develop the skill of verbalizing thoughts and desires, three techniques are particularly important: Reflective Listening, Trial-and-error, and Consequences. What your infant or young toddler says is not often as important as the need to continue having the youngster talk. In order to keep your young child talking, you need to reward him with your attention. Thus, the technique of Consequences (your attention is the reward or consequence) is essential. The technique of Trial-and-error is useful for helping your child make discriminations. Discrimination here means making a choice between what is acceptable and what is unacceptable. The toddler learns through trial-and-error that acceptable requests or ideas are met with something positive. Unacceptable verbalizations (Give me that!) are ignored.

Parents make a common error in trying too diligently to tell their child why what the child said was inappropriate or offensive. The consequence of paying excessive attention toward an inappropriate statement frequently is that your child feels rewarded. This is true despite the negative attention paid the child. A better tactic would be to use the technique of Ignoring. Ignoring will gradually reduce the offensive or inappropriate language.

Most professionals recognize that attention, either positive *or* negative, can act to reward a child's behavior. Yet, it is difficult to explain to parents that getting angry, yelling, or even spanking can serve to continue the child's misbehavior. After all, you would assume that your child would change his behavior if it is met with your displeasure.

An analogy which comes close to describing the attention phenomenon is this: an actor plays the role of a villain in a melodrama. An audience who "boos" the villain is rewarding the actor. That is what the actor expects. If the audience were to remain silent the actor, who is expecting a negative response, would be out of a job. Now substitute a child for the actor and parents for the audience. Parents paying (negative) attention to a misbehaving child are rewarding the child by fulfilling the child's expectation. If the parents were to ignore a child's misbehavior then the child would look for another part to play.

In effect, you provide the audience, with your child trying to maintain the audience's (your) attention. Your child can maintain the audience's attention by either playing a villain role or a good role. It makes sense that all you need to do is stop being a responsive audience in order to change your child's attention-getting behavior.

In order to help your child transmit a message, an effective tool is Reflective Listening. In your reflecting you can use more specific words and help your child clarify his point. For example, your child may say, "Can't we go?" Your reflective comment of, "You're feeling bored because there is nothing here for you to do," gives the child a more specific language to describe his thoughts. Through repetition the child learns to use a richer, fuller language.

Words that describe "feeling states" should be reflected when possible. Feeling states are those in which you can say, "I feel _____." Some feeling words are listed below:

sad	apathetic	delighted
angry	scared	disappointed
tense	spacey	overwhelmed
sour	afraid	despondent
ugly	hurt	light-headed
bored	ashamed	elated
happy	sleepy	cranky
irritable	panicked	

By reflecting these "feeling states" your child learns to match words to his feelings. He then can use language to more precisely explain his feelings. The ability to use language to cope with frustration, for example, is a major asset. Many of us feel bottled up with strong emotions because we are not able to voice the feelings. Examples of physical violence, such as wife beating or child abuse, can be a result of adults having no other way of expressing themselves. They could not adequately express themselves with language so they acted out their frustrations and angers directly on others.

A husband sought help for his marriage. Phil's wife, Georgia, left and took the couple's two young children. Phil reported the reason for Georgia leaving was that he slapped her on numerous occasions. When asked why he slapped Georgia, he said that he simply couldn't control himself when angry. Phil went on to describe several arguments which resulted in him slapping Georgia. The arguments had several elements in common: Phil was frustrated, he couldn't adequately explain his feelings or ideas to Georgia, and Georgia became impatient with Phil and talked instead of listening. After months of practicing, Phil learned to use words instead of physical force to express his angry feelings. His wife had resolved to obtain a divorce so Phil was unable to put his new skill to use with Georgia. He was, however, able to use it with a new girlfriend and even a co-worker on the job. The results were: no physical fights with the girlfriend (whom he later married), a cessation of fights at work, and a significant promotion. Several people including relatives told Phil that they felt they *understood* him better *now* and were more comfortable around him.

3. *Receiving a message.* The skill of receiving a message correctly has gained tremendous attention in recent years among psychologists and child-rearing experts. It is an extremely important subject despite its seeming simplicity. The reason for the attention is that listening has taken on a broader scope. It goes beyond passive sponge-like listening. Experts have used terms such as "active listening", "reflective listening", and "responsive listening" for this broader communication pattern. It means that a listener or responder must convince the speaker that what is said is really understood.

We probably all have had one-way conversations. The one-way conversation happens when one person is tuned out, daydreaming, or thinking about what they are interested in. It's the, "I might as well have been talking to a wall," feeling for the speaker. The divided-lane type of conversation is like two one-way conversations put together. One person is talking about their "thing". Both the one-way and divided-lane conversations are occurring all around us. Parties are particularly good settings to hear these two types of communications. Not much real understanding takes place. Few solid connections between people are made.

The speaker does not feel entirely satisfied unless he is confident that what he said was understood. In school, a

79

teacher can give a quiz or test to check out the level of understanding. But we can hardly go around quizzing everyone we talk with to see how much of what we say is fully comprehended. It usually becomes the job of the listener to make sure the conversation doesn't become one of the traffic-pattern forms of conversation mentioned above. Listening and absorbing are not enough. The next step is to reflect back to the speaker what was understood.

If someone asks you what time it is, then to respond with a reflective comment such as, "What you're asking me is to tell you the correct time of day," is obviously ridiculous. But, there are countless times when checking out or reflecting is the best bet. When little Jimmy asks why daddy can't live at home any more, or Mary says her best friend gets high on "grass" every day, these are good times to use reflective listening. Some good reflective responses are these: "Jimmy, I know you miss daddy and want him home;" and, "It sounds like you're very concerned about Debby." It will not be critical if you missed your child's intent the first time. Children will correct you if you are wrong.

A sizable portion of my counseling time is spent in having people reflect what was said to them. How do you get people, particularly children, to learn the reflecting skill? You should have guessed by now that modeling is an important first step. You need to continuously model reflective listening. Modeling cannot be stressed too much. Exposing your child to lots of good parental reflecting practically guarantees producing a good reflective listener. It will also insure less arguments, less confusion, and better understanding at home.

It is a fairly common practice to ask children to repeat instructions so we know they heard us. That's fine, but don't stop with instructions. If you say "no" to some request you may also want to ask, "Why do you think I'm saying 'no' to you?" Frequently, it is as important, or more so, for your child to understand the "Why?" behind your decision. Rather than continually telling him the "Why's" it may be best to ask him if he already knows the reasons. If parents asked that question more often, they would find that children understand much more about our reasoning than we think.

I succeeded in having a very concerned parent refrain from retelling his daughter about the company she kept. This father was fearful that his daughter was going to be led into mischief by wayward friends. It became an every other night event: he would mention to her something about her friends or what he was afraid would happen. The young teenager did a typical thing — she avoided home. She found all kinds of excuses to stay away, only upsetting her father more. Shirley's father, Rudy, complained to me that he felt his daughter did not understand what he was trying to tell her. The reader may remember this as a one-way conversation.

Rudy finally asked Shirley to explain back to him his feelings about her friends. Shirley masterfully told her father precisely the feelings he had, including a recap of the type of life he feared she would have. Rudy could hardly believe that Shirley actually understood what he, for years, was telling her. This father-daughter conflict had a delightful ending. Rudy, now convinced that his daughter was listening to him, stopped his long and frequent monologues. Shirley found fewer excuses to stay away from home. About three months after the initial conversation Shirley began a discussion about one of her friends — the one which Rudy was most concerned about. This time, Rudy was able to use reflective listening rather than his typical warning speech. During that conversation he found out that his daughter was seeing some faults the friend had. By continuing to reflect Shirley's feelings, Rudy successfully stopped putting Shirley in a position of defending the friend. A month after the second conversation, Rudy reported that his daughter had been going with several new and more acceptable (to Rudy) friends, looked happier, and talked more openly about her daily activities. Rudy was convinced that reflective listening worked.

In the beginning, parents complain that reflective listening is not normal or comfortable. They feel foolish restating what their children say. It does feel awkward in the beginning as with any new skill. It gets much easier with practice and much less mechanical. You may want to use one of the common lead-in phrases below:

What you're saying is ....

You're telling me that ....

Let's see if I understand. You're saying ......

What you're really telling me is ....

What you feel is ....

You mean that ....

Make your reflective response into a statement, not a question. This makes dialogue flow more smoothly. People are more uncomfortable with questions. Questions can sound as though you're being "set up". For example, if you used a reflective question such as, "Are you saying that you do want to visit Uncle Tim's?", the speaker may be on guard for your next comment. The fear may be that you will say, "But you said just last week that you didn't want to go visit Uncle Tim." We are constantly on guard, avoiding traps which make us look bad or seemingly catch us in a contradiction. We feel compelled to explain the apparent contradiction in a defensive fashion. We become irritated with "listeners" who are trying to put us in defensive positions. So, a safe form of reflecting is by stating what you think your child means. Given a chance, your child will always correct you if your interpretation is faulty.

4. *A discussion.* Ultimately, we prepare our children for adult conversations. Having an adult discussion involves sending thoughts and receiving messages as discussed earlier. Frequently though, discussions involve more than those two skills; it requires skill at resolving problems, finding areas of agreement or making joint decisions. Between spouses, at work, or even in social settings, there is a need to identify the source of conflict and work at overcoming differences. You can draw from a number of techniques to help in preparing children for these tasks: Negotiation, Humor, and Saving Face.

There are many opportunities to use negotiation as a means of resolving conflict. You should avoid consistent unilateral decisions. Using the technique of Negotiation over a wide range of parent-child conflicts, will prepare your child for adult-adult conflicts. Your child will have learned how to identify what the other side wants and ways of making compromises to secure some of what is wanted. Your child will also learn to waste less time on unresolvable areas.

By your use of Humor as a technique to deal with conflict, your child learns to imitate and insert humor into discussions. This is particularly true for unresolvable conflicts or when very strong feelings are encountered. Tactful humor can take the brutality and sting out of adult conflicts. Face saving comments are likewise good tension reducers. By saying, "You have a strong point there," or, "I can see you feel strongly about this issue," softens the clash.

As a summary, here are the important elements contributing to teaching communication:

Language development
Transmitting a message
Receiving a message
A discussion

An understanding of these elements and applying them will be extremely helpful in teaching your child to communicate.

CHAPTER 4
PARENTAL FEARS
OF ____

Child Rearing: What To Do Now

Parents have many fears of unknowingly doing damage to their children. "Experts" have told us contradictory things to the point that parents are understandably confused over what to do. Some fears which are particularly bewildering are: overprotectiveness, breaking the child's spirit, bribery, impulsivity, fairness and equality, physical punishment, and being too harsh. How significant is each fear? Below, each fear is discussed and ideas given to avoid the pitfall of extremes.

Being overprotective

It's just possible that as much damage is inflicted on youngsters by the overly protective or overly concerned parent as the neglectful parent. The neglected child can sometimes turn to others for support. When significant others are not available fantasy or various other coping mechanisms are employed. The neglected child has one advantage over the smothered child. The advantage is learning from errors (trial-and-error). The over protected child is prevented from seeing and experiencing the real or outside world. That child may not develop the confidence and self-esteem that comes from going ahead and making decisions. They learn to be highly dependent upon others; yet, they resent the dependency. I am not suggesting that parents forsake being overly-concerned only to be neglectful. What separates the "overly" from reasonably protective parent?

Healthy parents may be just as concerned about the welfare of their children as overly concerned ones. The difference lies in a *pattern* of actions that prevent or encourage independent thought and behavior. In the following descriptions keep in mind that what is being highlighted is a pattern of recurring parental behavior, not isolated examples. Any healthy parent may do and say the same thing as an overly protective one on a specific occasion.

Overly concerned parents tend to:
1. do things for children when children can and should do those things for themselves;
2. usually prevent children from making mistakes even when the mistake will not do any severe damage to the child;
3. usually make decisions for children when the child could reasonably make their own decision; the child learns to expect you to make decisions for him;
4. tell children what the results of any action or decision will be rather than letting him find out on his own;

5. continually ask children to account for their time;
6. don't often let children be away from them (for vacations, staying with a friend, etc.): the child lacks friends, stays home, and often follows you around;
7. play up or talk up the child's mistakes: in this way parents can justify making decisions for their children;
8. repeat the mistake of trying to talk children into behaving when talking doesn't work;
9. pay excessive attention to the child when the child is misbehaving (only to get attention).

A parent regularly relying upon one or more of the above policies results in a handicap for the child. The handicap is learned very early and sticks, despite efforts to overcome it.

Several signs to watch out for include your child always coming to you, expecting you to work out even small problems. Overly protective parents sometimes find their child throwing lots of temper tantrums. If you can't see the issues in perspective, others usually can. So consult friends, neighbors, and relatives. They can judge if your child is maturing adequately or is on the dependent side.

Breaking the child's spirit

An increasing number of parents are afraid to use discipline for fear of stifling their child's spirit. They fear that discipline will stifle the child's spirit of inquiry, adventure, and creativity. A parent does not want to transform their wild stallion into an old nag. We all tend to admire the unbridled freedom of a wild stallion and thrill at its success in breaking a halter. Thus, fear can dictate to parents a "hands-off" policy with their wild stallions (or mares, to be sure).

Is this a sensible policy? A simple answer to that question is "No," is not a sensible policy for children. We don't live in the same house as a wild stallion nor should we a wild child.

Inquiry, adventure, and creativity should be channeled. Creativity is more than a novel idea. If the novel idea doesn't fit or it's not appropriate then the idea isn't creative. The difference between genius and insanity is that while both have novel actions or ideas, one is appropriate and the other inappropriate. Therefore, the spirit needs channeling to be productive and civilized. A child can learn to exert spirit, but within reasonable limits. No one else will tolerate a wild child or adult so don't be afraid to use consistent, firm discipline.

Bribery

Bribery is wrong. But what exactly is bribery. Parents feel guilty for bribing and kids are supposed to rejoice in getting a sweet bribe. After all, shouldn't children learn how to behave and do their chores for the sake of the family, because it's their duty, or because they must learn to obey? Yet, kids surely don't start out that way!

Parent: "If I say that to Mike, isn't it bribery?"

Counselor: "Would you be working if they didn't give you money?"

Parent: "Yes, but I don't have to obey my boss. I expect my kids to mind me."

Counselor: "You don't always want to run your child's life; you want him to learn for himself, don't you?"

Parent: "Yes, I guess so."

Counselor: "By setting up a consequence you are helping him learn the consequences of his actions."

The above dialogue is a typical exchange. Counselors sometimes have difficulty explaining why, in certain situations, "giving something" is a bribe while at other times and situations it is recommended. Sometimes counselors play a semantic game by labeling. For example, bribes don't work, but rewards or reinforcements do work.

A counselor might describe how and when offering a bribe doesn't work. Bribes should *not* be given:

when the child is misbehaving;

when the desired behavior is a long time off (I'll give you $10 for each "A" you get on your report card.");

and when there is no chance for partial success.

Rewards or reinforcements work because:

misbehaving does not lead to a reward (as when a bribe is offered);

it is given soon after your child complies with your wishes; and

it is not a one time shot (even if he didn't make it the first time he can try again).

The real difference between bribes and rewards may not be in the type of problem but in the policy.

"Jenny, you can ask Pam to spend the night when you've finished your homework."

Is that a bribe or reward? Both, depending upon other details. At first glance, it sounds like Jenny is being bribed to finish her homework (bad). But if Jenny normally finishes her homework, then she is being given an unannounced reward (good). Or, if Jenny doesn't normally keep up with her homework and the agreed-upon policy was that whenever she caught up she could expect per-

91

mission to socialize, then she was offered a reinforcer (good).

One of the strong overriding issues throughout this book is that whatever a parent does rarely, occasionally or infrequently, will have almost no lasting effect on the child. Consistency produces a lasting effect. This idea leaves parents a wide margin for error. Therefore, if you bribe your child on rare occasions, it will not harm the youngster. It is only a concern when *frequent* bribing is practiced. How frequent is too frequent? That's a difficult question. Bribery is more of a problem with an unruly child than a generally compliant child, more a problem for temper-tantrum-throwing children than mellow children, and more a problem for a self-centered child than a generous child. For the more unruly, temper-tantrum-ridden and self-centered child the frequency of bribery should be kept to a bare minimum — perhaps no more than once per month. For children who are strongly compliant, mellow, and generous, I doubt it would be a matter of concern how frequently you "bribe" them.

Another general principal which follows the "rare occasion" idea is that if a bribe, incentive, or reward is given only once or a very few times, it is highly unlikely that sufficient learning has taken place. If a reward is going to be effective (teaching a habit), it needs to be given repeatedly. A good example of what is meant here is illustrated by the parents' desire to see higher school grades. Offering money for high grades at the end of the semester is an infrequent bribe. Children tend not to alter their studying for more than a few short weeks after the bribe is offered or just before report cards come out. The conclusion seems to be that since there is only infrequent repetitions of the reward then little learning or change takes place. Compare the above scheme with one which maximizes repetition of reward. In this alternative scheme a child is rewarded for each homework assignment, test, or quiz which is completed or given a high grade. The rewards may be much smaller and could even equal the size of the large reward which would have been given at the semester's end. Now there are many repetitions of the reward. Each day and each week there is something to gain, immediately, for better performance. One major difference in establishing the two schemes is that the one using repetition demands more time and effort from the parent. It will, nevertheless, offer greater benefits because it provides a more frequent and consistent pattern of encouraging school work. Remember that rewards are *not* always tangible such as money. Even if rewards start off being tangible, it is a good idea to shift toward non-tangible rewards such as a positive comment from you, or the internal rewards of getting good grades. Parents can measure their child-rearing success, in part, by the successful shift from tangible to non-tangible rewards.

When you think about the concept of bribery it is often a payoff for doing something that shouldn't be done. A prisoner may bribe a guard to keep quiet or to get him something normally unobtainable. A person getting a ticket may bribe the police officer to not write up the ticket. The payoff is to alter the normal, legal, ethical or moral code. Other payoffs are not seen as bribery. The boss who offers a bonus for outstanding performance and the company who offers a scholarship to an outstanding student are not seen as examples of bribery. Similarly, the judge who announces a prize for an art competition, the company who offers a double-your-money-back guarantee on a product, and the parole board who offers time off for good behavior to a prisoner are also not seen as bribing. The reason for the difference between what is considered bribery versus good policy is the emphasis on accepted practices. In this same way, your offering a payoff for consistently acceptable behavior should not be thought of as bribery.

Impulsivity

Many youngsters are labeled impulsive. As with many labels it can be good to have some of that quality (spontaneous), but too much (impulsive) or too little (dull) is undesirable. Impulsivity means that a child does something, usually an inappropriate behavior, before thinking through the possible consequences.

Impulsive:
Situation —— Action —— Consequence
Thoughtful:
Situation —— Pause to consider consequences ——
Action —— Consequence

An infant might be described as being impulsive because infants typically don't think of possible consequences. In order to put impulsivity under control, it has to be worthwhile for the child to *pause* before acting. Children who are consistently given second chances or warnings do not need to pause. They maintain the impulsive behavior.

The way to stop impulsivity is to provide immediate, swift, and, whenever possible, natural consequences. If your child "should have known" that his behavior was inappropriate, then a speedy, negative consequence becomes associated with the impulsive (inappropriate) action. Parents who do something immediately, such as sending the child to his room, a (soft) crisp slap, or sending him back to clean up the mess, report that the child begins to catch himself *before* an impulsive action, such as using bad language, yelling, throwing things, or misbehaving. Do not delay giving the consequence. If you delay the consequences, he will likely continue to be impulsive, followed, perhaps, by defensiveness, guilt or repentance.

The "pause" develops after many repetitions of encountering immediate, negative consequences for impulsive, inappropriate actions. The pause emerges as a self-protective device. Pausing may not necessarily change the action, but it will serve to make your child more thoughtful.

Too harsh a consequence for impulsive, inappropriate behavior is not the best way to curtail undesirable actions. Repetition of small to moderate negative consequences is better. This will allow more freedom to learn without unnecessary fear.

Fairness and Equality

The concepts of equality and fairness have taken on the aura of religious tenets. We strive through our courts and elected representatives to interpret and enact laws so that everyone may have an equal chance; equal opportunity under the law. Fairness and justice are near inseparable qualities which are preached to our youth. We try to insure that those in a state of early deprivation can get a head start.

This groundswell in support of fairness reaches its

supreme test in our homes and classrooms. Children receive the benefits of fairness by comparison with other siblings or schoolmates. Questioning of parents and teachers reveals the common reason for being fair: "Because it seems right. What would I say to others?"

Regardless of our fantasies and wishes there is only a limited degree of fairness and equality in our culture. We maintain an economic and political system that is not always fair and equitable. We can fool ourselves by saying capitalism and elections are fair. Everyone has a chance. No, our system is not completely fair and everyone doesn't have an equal chance. It is certainly more humane than chaos or totalitarianism but no governmental system is perfect. A major limitation is that people themselves are not fair and equal. People show favoritism, demonstrate unequal dealings with others, and use scapegoats instead of shouldering the blame.

It's natural to give preference to our relatives, friends, people we like or who strike us favorably. Consequently, we intentionally or unintentionally reject others, strangers, and those who look or behave differently than we do. To the politician or job applicant the world can be a cruel, harsh place which is not fair, does not give us a chance.

People, then, do disservice to rigidly teach equality and fairness to children who will be ill equipped for the unfair outside world. Legions of our graduates find a disappointing reality when their employer suddenly is not fair, when the work is boring, and when a bank looks at your income last year and doesn't give you the benefit of the doubt for a loan.

There are several good reasons *not* to be fair with

children. First, as I stated above, the world for which the child is being groomed is not always fair and equitable. Children need to experience dealing with unfairness and injustice. Secondly, children are not the same. They have unique needs which require that they are treated differently. Fairness does not mean "exactly the same". I prefer to think of fairness as "reasonableness". It is not reasonable to be perfectly equitable and just all the time. What may be a good policy for one child may be undesirable for another.

Don't worry about being fair!

Don't worry about treating each child identically!

Don't worry about justifying your not being fair!

It is usually the children whose parents have tried zealously to be fair and equitable that complain loudest of unfairness. To demonstrate the point let's compare the Weather and Strout families. The Weathers are third generation American; rather modern and suburban, they attended college and are active in the local PTA. The oldest boy Jeff is 14 followed by a pair of 11 year old twin girls. Arnold and Jean Weather are scrupulously careful to balance their attention, favors, and allowances between the children. Jeff, because he is older is given slightly more allowances but shares equally in responsibility.

The three children frequently argue unless gifts are shared and offered to all three at the same time. The kids are jealous of each other, particularly the twin girls. The girls Jean and Sarah don't like being treated identically but protest if the other sibling gets any slight advantage. All three kids show little respect for their parents and a variation of "you don't love me as much as _____" is on one of the three's lips daily. The Weathers find it difficult to satisfy the children for more than a short time before insults and rebuffs are heard.

The Strouts are a first generation American couple, having lived almost all their lives here. Neither of the elder Strouts completed high school and both continue to have trouble with the English language. Herman is a bricklayer. The Strouts have six children, three boys and three girls. While Herman favors the youngest girl, for which his wife Frances teases him, the Strout parents never seem to care whose turn it is. The parents keep only a skanty memory of whose turn it is to clean up messes, be assigned extra chores, receive a gift, or go on a walk with papa. Herman is "old-world" firm, which sometimes amounts to insulting a child or boxing an ear. These six children hardly ever argue, at least not with the intensity or frequency of the Weather children. I had fairly long talks with three of the six children and asked them if they thought their parents were fair with them. The answers seemed to reflect that each felt that if they needed or wanted something they stood a good chance of getting it, but they did not often need or want anything. All three mentioned that Christine was favored, but even this didn't seem to bother them. They understood that she was papa's favorite — that's the way it was.

The Strout children did have difficulties with papa because the father seldom complimented or encouraged his children. And the two families obviously differed in many more ways than keeping a strict balance sheet of fairness. The conclusion made when comparing the two families was that parents do not need to be overly concerned with being fair and possibly being too fair leads to conflicts. The Strout kids had less difficulty in accepting life's inequities than the demanding Weather children despite the fact that the Weathers were treated more equitably. There are enough examples of the Weather and Strout families to convince me that fairness does not always lead to harmony, nor is it the best preparation for adulthood.

Our culture has gone overboard in insisting on fairness in the home and classroom. Fairness has become such an obsession that it dictates how we treat our children. We make decisions not on what is best, but by the balance between children. I'm not suggesting that we allow our natural favoritism to run rampant. I am suggesting that you consider the unique needs of each of your children and respond to that need. Don't make excuses or feel guilty for treating the kids differently. Kids have different needs which must be met differently.

The interesting thing is that all too often your concern for fairness will be used against you. Children will manipulate you by saying you're not being fair. They will try to make you feel guilty so they can get their way. So, it's not fairness at all that is the issue. It becomes the ploy to accomplish selfish and greedy interests. Children can pressure you into making unreasonable decisions all in the name of fairness. Probably, if parents dropped the obsession of fairness they would make better decisions, better prepare children for life, become more aware of each child's unique needs, and rid themselves of unnecessary balance sheets and excess guilt.

Punishment
Spanking is usually discouraged by many experts in

parent-child relationships. Those experts suggest that you establish either positive or natural consequences for you child's actions rather than direct punishment. Avoiding spankings by using other techniques is ideal. But, if you are typical of most parents you will resort to physical punishment.

This author is not convinced that spanking is all bad if practiced "appropriately". I know of no convincing evidence that proves non-abusive spanking is harmful or damaging to children. Perhaps the most that can be said is:

There are other more effective techniques which can be used over a longer period of time (e.g., natural consequences, ignoring irrelevant behavior, and rewarding successful actions).

Spanking can be abused by parents (but so can other techniques).

For those parents who spank there are some helpful guidelines to follow:

1. To maximize the effect, spank immediately after the situation has occurred. If spanking is postponed, until you reach home or when father gets home, the punishment is not as closely tied to the misbehavior. Learning tends to be more effective if the consequence (spanking) is immediately administered. If the consequence is delayed then other undesirable behavior may take place. For example, the child, having nothing to lose, may continue misbehaving. The child may feel, "What the heck, if you're going to be reprimanded, you may as well really deserve it!"

2. Too severe of spankings tend to interfere with the

learning process. Children may resort to lying or sneaking. They may become so terrified of a spanking that normal development is altered. That is, children may become overly subservient, timid, and afraid to make decisions for fear of a terrible beating.

3. Too frequent of spankings tend to lose their value. Children may build up a tolerance for spankings; they become more immune to spankings. After a while, to get the same results you would need to almost resort to child abuse to get any response.

4. Don't give warnings before spanking. A quick, crisp smack on the behind or hand, without a warning, brings faster results. A big elaborate and prolonged spanking routine may not work as effectively. Don't threaten your child with a spanking. Either do it (spank) or provide another form of consequence.

Punishment can be described as a parent exerting *control* over a child by imposing a *consequence* . The two italicized words are key concepts. You may not always want to exert control directly. You may choose to allow your child to learn from his mistakes by "nature taking its course". In effect, you do not always want to impose punishment for wrong-doing. Sometimes, wrong-doing has a way of providing its own consequence, without your intervention. The second key word "consequence" suggests that punishment can be different from a spanking, swat, slap, or being sent to one's room. The concept allows you to be creative in finding an antidote for the undesirable behavior. You are free to select a remedy that will do

the best job without always having to physically punish.
The best remedies tend to be:
1. Going back and doing it right.
2. Taking responsibility by cleaning up the mess.
3. Telling the child that you are disappointed (sad, furious, hurt, etc.) by his actions.
4. Consistent and immediate.
Examples of more creative ideas (instead of punishment) are:
1. For children who sleep in their sleeping bags despite being told to sleep in bed (children may do this to avoid making the bed): Have the children wash the sleeping bags as frequently as you would wash the sheets. One "hand-washing" in a tub may do the trick!
2. For children who cut classes: You sit through class with your child to make sure he stays there. Imagine the embarrassment your child will undergo!
3. For the child who marked the wall with ink or crayons: The child cleans the wall. If that doesn't get the color off he helps paint the wall. Young kids may not do a perfect job but they should put out the effort.
4. For bedwetters: Depending upon age, the child strips the bed, changes sheets and washes out the soiled sheets.
5. For the nonstudier: Hire an older neighbor child to serve as a tutor. It is amazing how much work can be accomplished by a diligent teenager tutor in an hour per night, five nights a week.
6. For children who leave lights on: An "electric" fee

is charged. Five cents for each caught instance — payable immediately. Coversely, helping to reduce utility costs can be rewarded.

Being too Harsh

Here are some rough guidelines to assess how commanding or harsh you are:

Do your punishments (for example, restrictions) frequently last more than one week?

Does your child avoid staying home?

Is your child rather quiet?

Does your child rarely ask you for advice or initiate conversations?

Does your child rarely test out your rules?

Does your child never throw temper tantrums (if he is young)?

A positive response to any one of the above does not imply harshness. If there is a trend toward "yes" answers then you may be on the harsh side.

I have found that harsh parents who tend to be inconsistently harsh (outbursts of being very strict followed by excessive leniency) meet with more opposition and resistance than parents who tend to be consistently harsh. Some child "experts" believe that being harsh inhibits your child's free expression, stifles creativity, and forces your child into indirect expressions of anger. Sometimes that is accurate. However, some of the healthiest kids come from strict families. It may be that strictness or harshness is not the only important factor. More important than degree of harshness may be elements such as consistency, understanding, humor, and degree of independence. These are the dimensions that provide stability. Inconsistency teaches your child not to trust in you. Children who clearly know the limits or boundaries are more content, regardless if those limits are strict or are on the lenient side.

The issue of stifling creativity may not be a function of strictness. A parent can be strict yet allow a large degree of independent thinking. It's only when you want to control your child's thinking that you become stifling. If being strict or harsh means your child can't make a move without your permission then yes there is a problem. But, if you are strict or "overly" punitive on certain clearly defined tasks then your child will learn the ropes. Obviously there should be limits on harshness as well as on permissiveness. Within those two extremes, however, we really don't know what is best in the long run. For this reason I tend to be more concerned with the other dimensions such as consistency which do seem to make a difference.

CHAPTER 5.
TYPICAL PARENT
COMPLAINTS:
WHAT DO I DO NOW?

Child Rearing: What To Do Now

While you may feel you are having unique problems with your child it is astonishing how common the complaints really are. Below are typical complaints that parents have. Corresponding to each complaint there are some ideas and directions that may be useful. For convenience, the specific complaints are grouped into four general headings: "Getting children to assume responsibilities", "Sibling rivalry and social offenses", "Bad attitude", and "Miscellaneous issues".

Getting children to assume responsibilities

The complaints often heard from parents regarding children not taking responsibility are these:

"I have to yell at him/her constantly."

"He/She never completes a job."

"My child forgets frequently."

"I have to remind him all the time."

"They will do it only if I stand over them."
"My child is lazy."
"He/She does poorly in school."
Each of these complaints are discussed in detail with ideas, remedies or suggestions for the parent to try.

"I have to yell at him/her constantly." This is a frustrating situation. It seems that the more you yell the more you need to yell. Your child tends not to listen *until* you yell. Consider some of the following ideas:

1. Give fewer requests or orders. Get it down to a manageable number to focus on.

2. Identify a preestablished consequence that will happen for noncompliance. Review the technique of Consequences starting on page 26.

3. Consequences may be going back and (re)doing the task. Staying in the kitchen, bathroom, or bedroom until the dishes are done, hands are washed, or the room is cleaned are all excellent consequences. Make the inconvenience fall on your child for noncompliance, not on you.

4. Do not repeat yourself; avoid reminders. Let the consequence do the teaching. I am going to repeat that idea because it is the essence of easy child-rearing. *Let the consequence do the teaching.* If you trust in the consequence, avoiding reminders and repeated requests, you are less likely to get worked up and yell. You can patiently let your chosen consequence work its magic.

5. It would be a good idea to start with one "chore rule" and get it under control. Follow the technique of Rules on page 23. Such chores as doing dishes, cleaning a room, feeding animals, trash

removal, and doing lawn work are good everyday tasks to start with.

6. Expand to other tasks gradually. Make sure your child is in the habit of accomplishing the one task before adding new ones. Maintain one task for at least two months before adding to it.

7. Yelling will distract from the "target" task you want your child to accomplish. As a result of this distraction you may complete the job yourself. It may not seem worth the fuss to get him to do the task. This tactic results in the child ignoring your yelling because there is no other consequence. You're all wind and your child knows it. Always identify a consequence for *you* to enforce even if it is only standing quietly by until the job is done.

"He/She never completes a job." The assumption here is that your child is testing your persistence. He may think he will get partial credit and be excused from finishing the entire task. All that is required to cope with this problem is stick to the criterion of total completion of the task. Particularly with routine tasks, have your child go back and (re)do what did not measure up to your standard. It won't take many rewashes of dishes, recleaning hands and face, or revacuuming a room to get the message across. Don't get into the habit of allowing children to squeak by. Make an issue of each task. It is time consuming in the beginning but it will get easier later on.

"My child forgets frequently." This situation makes you wonder if there is something physically wrong with your child. Generally, forgetting takes place in a conducive environment. Consider the following ideas:

1. Does your child get rewarded occasionally by forgetting? This means, does your child escape from

doing the task? She may not need to get out of the task every time. After all, to continue gambling you don't need to win on each throw of the dice. You may win or come close to winning just often enough to keep trying.

2. You need to follow through on each and every request you make. So, limit the number of requests to as many as you can comfortably enforce.

3. Make it inconvenient for your child to forget by establishing consequences for forgetting. You don't need to add punishment. All you need to do is see to it that it is inconvenient to forget. Examples are: sitting down to a cold meal because your child needed to complete the task before dinner. The family went ahead and ate while the child finished the task. Don't be afraid to wake your child up and have him complete a task that should have been finished before bedtime. If he is in a rush to go somewhere he will have to wait until that "forgotten" task is finished before leaving. Having him walk back to school to get the forgotten book is a good consequence for forgetting.

4. You may have doubts whether your child actually forgot or deliberately forgot. It does not really matter which is true. You must follow the same procedure. You may never know which is true. If you make it consistently inconvenient for the forgetful child you will notice how quickly he learns to remember. You do not need to be a mindreader to know if the child actually or deliberately forgot. Go ahead and supply the consequence. The consequence should be relatively mild, yet unpleasant

enough to teach him the benefits of remembering. *"I have to remind him all the time."* Frequent reminders shift the responsibility from the child to you. That is, you're still stuck with the responsibility of making him aware of the chore. The result is that a normal child will ignore the responsibility until reminded. He does not remind himself because you do that for him. Therefore, you induce irresponsibility and forgetting with reminders. What can be done about this situation? You might say, "But if I don't remind him he won't do it." Again, the answer is simple. Let the consequence do the teaching. If you neglect to remind, your child will experience the consequence. The consequence will do the teaching and reminding. There are many possible consequences which are not overly harsh but are powerful enough to inconvenience a child. Through repetition he learns what to expect and will remind himself. Some examples of consequences may be: If not in bed by 9:00 PM the child, tomorrow, loses his extra ½ hour to stay up. Or, if all ready for bed (teeth brushed, clothes changed, etc.) then the child earns an extra ½ hour to stay up.

Natural consequences such as going to school in winter without a jacket or losing a possession because of negligence, are excellent teaching devices. One parent was concerned about her son's teeth. The boy never brushed, with the result being mom constantly reminded him. An excellent consequence was that he could go out to play or watch TV after the teeth were brushed. This parent bought "disclosure" stain which left a temporary discoloration on the teeth where the boy had not brushed well. It was an easy task for the child to prove he brushed by using the disclosure stain. He then could go out to play.

111

The parent just needed to prevent the boy from leaving the house or watching TV until proof of brushing. The parent monitored the boy not by reminding him to brush his teeth but by saying, "you can't watch TV yet", by saying, "What was the rule?", by turning off the TV, or by calling the child back after he escaped and waiting until he remembers about brushing. The child quickly learned to remind himself and avoided the inevitable of going back to brush. If there is no escape the child will learn the most expedient path. He does not like to be delayed from playing or watching TV.

Remember, reminders serve to encourage more reminders. It becomes an endless waste of your time.

"They will do it only if I stand over them." This common complaint is heard from teachers as well as parents. One of the principal reasons for children ignoring the task until mother, father, or teacher looks over their shoulder is a negligent pattern of rule enforcement. You may be in a habit of assigning a task then walking away. After a while you discover the unfinished task and remind your child. Another delay occurs until frustration sets in, followed by standing over the child. The child has learned that people only mean business when they stand over him. If they don't stand over him then he is at liberty to ignore the task.

Here are several ideas to consider:

1. Assign tasks or chores in such a way that the job must be completed *before* moving on to play or any other activity. The child's world stops until the task is finished.
2. In the early stages of training (which may last for years) you should continuously monitor your

child's activity. He must stay at the task without getting completely distracted. For example, having him stay in the kitchen until the dishes are completed or in his room until clothes are picked up is excellent. You should monitor so that he doesn't sneak out to watch TV or some other diversion.

3. Arrange the task so that time is on your side. Allow time to be the punisher. By setting up the chore so that he can stay at a task for an indefinite time period you can put boredom on your side. If the task must be completed before dinner, watching TV, or going out to play, then don't get impatient for the job to be completed. If the child wastes time, let him. If he takes hours to do a five-minute job it wastes his time, not yours. Why should you get upset if he wastes his time; after all, it's his choice to waste time and he is the one suffering. If the task is to clean the bathroom then have him stay in the bathroom until the job is totally finished. If this job takes all evening and it's bedtime, OK. Allow him to go to sleep. But, tomorrow he goes back into the bathroom for another long boring evening.

Children get tired of doing nothing. They get bored and want to have fun. By taking advantage of time, you will teach children to get the job over with quickly. They will realize that it is no advantage for them to delay.

4. Repetition is a good teacher; use it. If you are consistent your child knows what to expect. By employing the above ideas routinely, your child will come to know that "getting on" with the task is the only good solution.

113

5. Form the habit of leaving him alone to do the task. All you need to do is be near enough to make sure he remains where he is supposed to. You may be required to send him back to him room, kitchen, or wherever. Do this with as few words as possible. You don't want to distract him with talking. He knows what to do. It's your job to make sure he doesn't escape until the work is finished.
6. There may be times when standing over the child is an effective and forceful technique. This policy should be used for confrontations when it is best not to talk. But the procedure of standing by until the job is finished should be used in more dramatic confrontations rather than during routine chores.

"My child is lazy." He won't do anything unless I tell him to. Being lazy is a habit which provides certain benefits, at least in the short run. Children learn to be lazy and find that assuming a lazy posture gets them out of numerous chores. Most parents will admit that they have refrained from giving the "lazy" child chores and responsibilities because it produces too many arguments. Who wants to struggle constantly? So the child does get rewarded. He gets out of doing work. He may appear lazy but the child's actions are actually adaptive; he's coping with his world the best way he knows how.

How can laziness be changed?

1. It is a long process. The older the child the more difficult to break the habit.
2. Begin with one chore that will be a long-standing responsibility. It is you, the parent, who needs to be persistent at monitoring and providing the established consequences. Review the technique of

Rules, page 23.
3. Be consistent and don't allow the child to slip back. Don't allow more than one or two excuses in a month for a daily chore unless the child is hospitalized or has an equally good excuse.
4. Add more responsibilities gradually without excusing or forgetting to enforce the previous ones. No more than one new responsibility per one or two months should be introduced.
5. Lazy children are often experts at wasting time. Put this to your advantage. You shouldn't be disturbed if your child takes all evening to wash the bathtub, all day to mow the lawn, or a whole weekend to clean the room. Let the child sit there, bored, until the job is finished. This means no TV, stereo, or playthings. When will all that boredom stop? When he completes the assigned task. He then becomes frustrated with being lazy. I haven't seen many children willing to stay in the kitchen more than about four or five hours before the dishes get done. What happens if you have a particularly trying child? He stays in the kitchen the second day, beginning immediately after school. It's his time he's wasting. Again, be patient and allow time to work for you.

"He/She does poorly in school." Generally, I find that children who are capable, but negligent at schoolwork are also negligent at home. You might label it "shirking responsibility". If you have the problem of your child getting D's or F's in school, ask yourself if he does chores regularly at home. If the answer is that he is not performing home chores without many reminders, then the place

115

to begin is at home. Review the sections on setting a Rule (page 23) because you will want your child to get into a habit of doing some work. Only after he is regularly doing several home chores without needing to be reminded, should you focus on the schoolwork. Consider the following steps:

1. Talk with your child's teacher(s). The teacher is a valuable source of information about your child.
2. Try to talk with the teacher at a noncrisis point such as at the beginning of school. Talking with teachers at a crisis point often puts teachers on the defensive. The teacher may try to focus excessively on the crisis (for example, a poor grade on a particular paper or some behavioral problem) rather than helping you to reach a positive plan. Teachers are "human" and in my experience are frequently uneasy (on guard) when talking to parents.
3. One of the best procedures I have found is to have the teacher assign daily homework for your child. If the youngster has several teachers pick one to give regular homework. The assignments can start off fairly short — a half hour perhaps. The main point is to have it assigned daily. Usually it is best to begin with work you can easily check as opposed to a straight reading assignment that is much more difficult to check. It is *your* job to see that the homework is done; it is not necessary for the child to do all the work correctly. Let the teacher focus on the correctness of the work.
4. There should be no excuses for forgetting to bring home an assignment. If there is still time send the child back to the school for the book. If it is too late

then you can either supply equivalent schoolwork (such as math problems that are appropriate) or extra chores. It should be fairly unpleasant for the child to "forget". An hour or two of some alternative work should serve to discourage forgetfulness.

5. It is not necessary that the homework count toward the child's grade. The only concern is that it is relevant to current work in class. Some teachers fiercely oppose giving a child grade credit for this specialized work. That's fine. The work will eventually result in higher grades. It's the habit that counts.

6. You may meet teacher resistance toward this plan. Teachers, like parents, are obsessed with fairness. They may feel it is "unfair" to give your child extra homework when no one else is getting it. If this is a problem you must be firm. Your child's education is ultimately your responsibility. You may want to pick another teacher to talk with if you meet resistance from one teacher. The principal can be another resource.

7. A teacher is very likely to forget an occasional assignment. Make your child responsible for asking for assignments even if the teacher forgets. How? Regardless of who forgets, have the child do the added, alternative work.

8. Keep in frequent contact with the teacher, particularly in the beginning. The motto of, "If anything can go wrong, it will," is apt. Don't be afraid of pestering the teacher. A good contact schedule is to call or see the teacher at least twice during the first week that assignments are started. If all is going

well then cut back to once-a-week contact for the next three weeks. Then gradually less frequent thereafter, but never less than one contact per month for the first year. These contacts will keep the teacher particularly interested in your child's progress. The teacher will know he has an ally in you and feel more at ease sharing important observations with you. You should also check with the teacher to see if your child turned in the work and is keeping up with daily in-class work.

9. You may want to broaden the schedule to include other subjects and teachers. Do this only after the first program has become a habit. It may take from a month to three months for the habit to be established. Don't rush; there's plenty of time. Build on success, gradually and deliberately.

10. You should schedule a homework deadline. This can be immediately after school (although many parents prefer this to be play-time), before supper, or right after dinner. It is probably best not to make it before bedtime. Due to unavoidable delays for all sorts of reasons it may be best to make the time limit earlier. At first your child may be slow at completing the work. As long as there are no distractions he will learn to finish more quickly. He may, in the beginning, try to "out delay" you, but you can be more persistent in sticking to the plan. Remember, no distractions such as TV, radio, or games.

11. You *must* check to verify that the homework is completed (*all* completed) before your child is released to eat dinner, play, go out, or whatever.

Avoid showing your impatience or temper. Just send him back to finish the homework. Completed does not mean correct. Make sure that the effort is there, though.

12. Another technique is to reward the child for getting good grades. I am more enthusiastic about this technique for younger children than older ones, but it should improve any child's schoolwork. By the time a child reaches the teens many parents see rewarding good grades as offensive. They resent "paying-off" the child for the child's obligation. I shall not argue with that position but only tell you the technique.

13. Rewards, whether in the form of points toward something, money, special privileges, or whatever, should be given for each and every test, graded homework, quiz, paper, or class assignment. This is preferable to waiting until the term ends and a final grade is issued. What you'll be doing is encouraging higher grades step by step throughout the term. The more immediate the reward the greater the effort will be to get better grades.

14. If you offer points, ultimately redeemable for something, you will want to offer a range of possible scores. For example, you may decide to give 10 points for an "A", 8 points for a "B", 5 for a "C", 2 for a "D", and 1 for an "F". You can alter the point values to suit your need. The reason for the range is that your child can get some points for his performance and more for better performance. It is not an "all or nothing" situation. You may even want to give some credit for an "F".

Why? Because at least you will see those papers. If no credit is given, the child may throw the "F" papers away. Set the point total low enough so some goals can be quickly reached. Gradually make the goals worth higher point values. It can be fun and sometimes a challenge to assign point totals for particular goals. How many points would it take to go bowling with dad, see a movie, go out to eat, buy a special ring, play a game with mom, or sleep over at a friend's house? Again, these games tend to work better with younger children than older ones.

Sibling rivalry and social offenses

Parental concerns regarding sibling rivalry and social offenses center on the following complaints:

"They fight constantly."

"He's so selfish; he won't share."

"He's a bully."

"He uses dirty words."

"He refuses to do things I ask (tell him to do)."

"My son has been stealing from me."

"My child lies to me."

"They never want to stay home."

The format is to examine each complaint, supplying helpful directions.

"They fight constantly." Many parents are concerned with their children's fighting. They want the kids to get along together without fighting. Parents also try to equalize the squabbles or serve as a mediator. Yet, it appears that the more diligent you are in resolving sibling conflicts the more the conflicts persist. The frazzled parent

Typical Parent Complaints: What do I do now?

spirals from mediator to punisher only to find a new conflict to mediate. What can you do? Below are five ideas to help out:

1. Stay out of sibling conflicts. I can suggest several theories of why this policy works to reduce conflicts. But they are only theories and I have attempted to avoid theories here. In all, save an extremely few unusual situations, having parents ignore sibling conflicts serves to reduce future conflicts.

2. Tell the complaining sibling, "You will have to settle it between yourselves" or "I bet that made you mad." Don't even try to find out who is right or wrong. Ignore the conflict.

3. On a handful of occasions it may be useful to consult with the complaing child. Consulting basically means asking him to identify options or possible courses of action. For example, if big brother took the younger's prized possession and won't give it back, what tactics can the younger child identify to overcome this problem. Help him identify several alternatives and possible consequences. The younger child could stand up and fight, plead with the older bully, retaliate, or ignore the older child. Ask him, "Is there anything else you can do?" in order to solicit his ideas. You want the child to discover possible solutions and try them out. If one solution does not work he will need to try another. All the time, however, you are *not* suggesting what to do or directing his actions. It's a trial-and-error process with the child in control.

4. When you begin to ignore sibling conflicts you

should anticipate an overdose of fights. You might also notice the children trying strongly to enlist your assistance. They might scream louder or cry harder or fight more frequently. Be patient. In a few days, several weeks at the longest, there will be a change for the better.

5. Rarely does one child deliberately and seriusly hurt a sibling. If you have one of these very rare children you should seek professional help. Typically, if someone gets hurt you will find the guilty child already feeling horrible. The experience of inflicting real pain (needing medical attention) is a powerfully sobering sight for a child. Further punishment is not helpful. In fact, saying something such as, "I guess you feel awfully bad about what happened", is helpful in easing the guilt.

"He's so selfish; he won't share." Many people value sharing and want their children to have that value. When they find that their children do not share with siblings or friends it upsets parents and they try to actively change the pattern. Sharing is a complex task to learn. Imagine the infant in its total selfishness. The transition from an infant's selfishness to sharing is a slow one. Here are some guides that help in making that transition:

1. How well do you serve as a model for sharing? Do you share fully with others? Modeling is the best first step in teaching sharing. For very young children you can say, "Mother is sharing her ____ with Jenny." At another time you can say, "Does Jenny want to share her ____ with mother?" This of course goes beyond simple modeling but it is effective with very young children. Parents must model

sharing with others to set the example. This point was discussed previously on page 66 under the heading "Being generous".

2. For the typical American culture certain property rights are respected. One plan to follow is to give your child possession over certain things such as playthings and clothes. Obtain permission whenever you do anything with those possessions. If you model this policy your child will eventually imitate you and ask before using your possessions.

3. Another argument for giving the child dominion over certain possessions is that it teaches the result of selfishness. If the child is selfish then others will return that selfishness.

I saw a family with three preteens. The parents felt strongly about sharing but the children were constantly fighting over possessions. The parents reacted by declaring everything public property (ownership by all members equally). The result was an escalation in the arguments. The parents were frequently called in to settle who had what first and who grabbed it away. The parents decided to punish both — the taker for not respecting who he took the object from and the original possessor for not sharing freely (for hoarding). This policy *added* to the conflicts. Tempers were always near the surface.

As I suggested earlier (page 67) my first step with the family was to ask each child to make a complete list of things he or she felt he owned. I then read each child's list out loud to the family. In doing so I proclaimed that everything on the list was the sole and exclusive possession of that child. Anyone else, including parents, must ask permission to hold or use any private possession. I then sent the family home fully expecting what happened; I had forewarned the parents of what was to come. There was absolutely no sharing of possessions in the first week by two of the children and only minor sharing by the youngest child. After reassuring the bewildered parents, we continued into the second week. What the parents reported was that there emerged a type of primitive, strict exchange system. One thing was loaned only on the condition another was shared. At first the children kept a careful record and each could recite what concessions were given for what favors. As the weeks passed the two younger children exchanged more freely and lost track of the balance sheet. The older child held out and continued to be rather selfish. This condition, however, presented the older child with various problems. The other two were reluctant to share because of the difficulty in arriving at a mutually satisfactory settlement. Therefore, for a time the older child was excluded from many play activities by the younger ones. This is a "natural consequence" and proved useful. During the fifth week the older child began showing signs of frustration. When the parents pursued their policy of noninterference the older child began offering his possessions to the other two "free of charge". He dropped the favor-for-a-favor system in order to regain friendship ties. The parents also noted an increase in sharing between their children and peers outside of the home.

The process in the above sketch was to give children something to possess. Once in control, the child will naturally find advantages in sharing. This self-discovery of the advantages gained by sharing will gradually transform into more stable habits. Incidentally, by the same

process children can learn when it is not best to share.
4. Look for games and tasks which require sharing. Many such opportunities occur. Doing dishes can obviously be a shared task — one washes, the other dries. If the washer is very slow it burdens the dryer. When these tasks are reversed the new washer may return the frustration. There will be arguments and squabbles. By parents avoiding interfering in sibling conflicts the arguments become productive. These arguments will lead to better bonds between siblings. There are many games which require two participants: teeter-totter, ping-pong, tennis, badminton, and card games. Sharing can be enhanced by setting relay races (running or swimming), three-legged contests, and taking-turn games. An example of a taking-turn game is drawing. One child can draw certain colors while the other takes turn with other colors. Variations on drawing games can be for one to draw portions of a body, figure, or picture with the other child drawing other portions.

It takes extra thought to invent sharing games because our culture emphasizes individual success. But with persistence you can find sharing activities that are fun for the children.
5. There is a natural inclination for parents who value sharing to become angry at seeing selfishness in their children. This anger becomes translated into temper outbursts, morality lectures, punishment, and attempts toward enforcement of sharing. Generally, the more a parent insists upon sharing the more children resist or ignore you. The values your

child acquires are usually the unspoken life style rather than what is thrust upon them. Avoid enforcing a sharing process through anger or threats. *"He's a bully."* Bullying is learned. How? Probably by trial-and-error. A strong-arm approach or a demand is tried and it works. Since it worked once it will be tried again. Bullying can take the form of physical threats, assaults, blackmail, or teasing. Here are some ideas to consider:

1. Some bullies are imitating a parent. If one parent is overbearing or dominating and the other is rather submissive then a child may attempt to imitate the dominant parent. He may try to use this tactic against the submissive parent and may find that it sometimes works. Sigmund Freud talked about "identification with the aggressor" as one process in child development.

   We are hearing more and more about how child abuse and wife battering are passed along from parent to child. So, it is important to first examine your role and set a good example.

2. A bully may try to wield power at home. Rather than serve as an inappropriate model and loudly or violently punish the young bully you may want to react by ignoring the demands.

3. If your child is trying to gain attention by using force or bully tactics, then it will be helpful to give attention when he is *not* being a bully. The attention may be given when your child has been alone and quiet rather than when he is loud and attention-seeking. Give positive attention particularly when he is with other kids and they are getting

along well. In effect, be positive and praise when the behavior you want is observed rather than punish for the bullying.

4. Most times a child learns as a result of natural consequences. The natural consequences for bullying is for kids to avoid playing with or associating with the bully. If parents do not interfere, this natural process usually results in lots of loneliness for the bully. This process is most effective with young children. By about twelve years of age the pattern is much more difficult to curtail through natural consequences. Why? Because the bully may have acquired friends who also bully or friends who submit to the bullying. Also, by that age the pattern has probably been effectively reinforced by other children cowering in fear.

5. If most of the undesirable behavior occurs outside of home, it may be a good idea to enlist the aid of teachers, parents of the child's friends, and various leaders that see the bully child outside the home. A teacher may be able to isolate (send out of the room) the bully whenever the undesirable behavior begins. Other parents may encourage their children to avoid the bully. In this way more pressure is brought upon the child to drop the bullying behavior.

"He uses dirty words." Using unacceptable language is a variation of unacceptable behavior. As with the other unacceptable actions, dirty words can be effectively ignored. If your child sees you wince, scowl or turn red it may turn into a game for the child. Therefore, you must totally ignore the words for ignoring to be effective.

127

There are several other techniques to use with dirty words. One technique is what educators and psychologists call a "time-out" procedure. This procedure is precisely what grandma did when she sent Jimmy to his room. Does the technique work? You bet! Make sure to do it *immediately* after you hear the selected word(s); don't say anything more. If you send Jimmy to his room after the 10th word you just allowed 10 words to go by without action, thus condoning 10 words you disapprove of. Jimmy will get tired of going to his room and will eventually think before he says another dirty word. Give it time, though; be patient.

Some psychologists have suggested to reward the absence or reduction of dirty words. For example, if the child who is used to saying 50 dirty words per day (in your presence) reduces the number to 25 or 30 then there is a reward given (or points toward a reward) that day. A chart is often kept to record the child's progress. Clearly, the reward must be enough of an incentive for the child to think about reducing his use of dirty words. If the frequency of dirty words is low, it is possible to reward the total absence rather than just cutting down. Psychologists see this procedure different from bribery because, once the incentive is in force, there is no benefit to the child to be naughty. In bribery, a child can solicit a bribe by being bad. While this technique does work, it rubs most parents the wrong way. They don't like the approach, feeling that they are paying off children who cuss.

"He refuses to do things I ask (tell him to do)." There are lots of ways to get children to abide by your requests. First, ask yourself how many requests you are already making. Are they all necessary? If you can reduce the

total number you'll be ahead. If you can't reduce the number try grouping them together rather than spreading the requests throughout a day. You may even want to write them down and post them. Are the requests repetitive? If this issue is a problem try using one or more of the ideas below:

1. For young children, there are effective ways of turning the request into a game. "Let's see how fast we can pick up all the toys." Use a timer or count out loud. Make the task sound fun. Sing a song while doing a chore with the child. If you sound excited, positive, and happy your young child will pick up your enthusiasm. Being pleasant sure helps. Give it a try.

2. Again for young children, take him in hand and force him to finish the task. It is time-consuming, aggravating, and frustrating, but if done *consistently* your young child will stop testing you to see if you mean business. No warnings. After the first request has been ignored take him in hand and get the job done. This comes as a surprise — an unpleasant one — which the young child does not like. Keep your words to a minimum; sound and look determined.

3. Provide a time limit for each request. Try to give the youngster a few minutes to finish whatever he is doing. Yet, don't give too long a limit. A day for a young child is too long; a week for most preteens is too long a limit also. If the entire task cannot be completed within fairly short limits, break the task up into parts which can be accomplished within short time periods.

Time limits can be before dinner, bed time, immediately after school, before going out to play, by 1 PM, 6:30 PM, when the sun sets, when the street lights go on, after that TV program, in 10 minutes, 2 hours, or any recognizable time or event.

One father whom I saw in counseling gave his son permission to go out and play for about 20 minutes after dinner on a daily basis. The boy, nine years old, frequently did not return within the time limit. The father usually went out to look for his son about 10 to 15 minutes *after* the deadline. When he found the boy he brought him in and scolded him. The father complained that he could not trust his son — because he didn't return within the time limit.

In understanding the above dilemma you need to assess a nine-year-old's ability to keep track of 20 minutes of elapsed playtime. I would not expect kids at that age to keep accurate measurements of time. One solution was to give the boy a watch, or better yet a timer set for 20 minutes. At the end of 20 minutes if the boy has not returned the father looks for him. He doesn't wait an extra 10-15 minutes before looking. In this case the father was instructed to say nothing beyond, "How long were you allowed to play?" when he located his son. The next day at playtime father could set the timer to 10 minutes instead of 20 as a penalty for the previous days mistake. Sometimes the penalty is not needed but was used in this case as an added incentive to come home before father goes searching.

The procedure worked well with the boy having missed a total of 20 minutes of playtime in the first three weeks of the program. This procedure worked because the deadline was more understandable for the child (the triggering of a timer), father's searching immediately at the time limit, and the repetition and consistency of father's enforcement of the policy.

4. Standing over your child, waiting for him to finish a task is another simple, old fashion technique. For this to be effective you must not say anything, only wait and appear stern. Everyone's "world" stops until the task is finished. This technique can be very effective with older children who try to postpone compliance. It should be done without second chances and without words if possible.

5. For a child who is compliant with most requests you can ask, "What were you to do?" or, "What did I ask?" The question should not be a shout; it should be a determined stand. It also should not be repeated. This procedure can be followed by number 2 or 4 above. But, don't say it and walk away, thus enabling the child to again ignore you! Stand firm and appear ready for a confrontation.

6. Try making something you child wants "conditional" upon complying with your request. For example, "When you mow the lawn (clean your room, dust, vacuum, water the plants, or hang the clothes on the line) you can go out to play (eat dinner, watch TV, read the book, lay down, or play a game with me)." It is best to make the treat logically follow the required task. Earning an extra ½ hour

can be logically connected to getting to bed without fuss the night before. The extra time becomes a reward for compliance with a precise bed time.

7. Making use of "time" is similar to item 6 above. This slight variation is making "escape" contingent upon compliance. When the job is completed the child can go free. Until the job is accomplished *and inspected* he remains at the task. He stays in the kitchen until the dishes are done, in the bathroom until it is clean, outside until the car is washed, in his room until cleaned, in the tub until washed, and so forth. Eventually he will want to escape this confinement and will do the job more quickly. Through repetition the job will be completed sooner and sooner, especially if there is something he wants to do afterward.

8. If the chore is a frequent one, it may be best to set a rule regarding the chore. You should review the technique of Rules on page 23.

"My son has been stealing from me." You should become concerned when you find your child regularly stealing from you or others. An occasional theft is understandable and is most often followed by lots of youthful guilt and repentance. But when it becomes a habit what can be done?

1. An assessment of property rights is in order. Are you, as parents, setting up the model of "Everything that is mine is mine and everything that is yours is mine?" It would then be natural for your child to mimic your actions and disregard others property rights. Therefore, provide your child with his own possessions. Be a good model.

2. Provide your child with ways of earning money. The child might earn all his spending money by doing special chores.

   I am not suggesting that you "pay off" your child for doing routine chores. There are always difficult or unusual tasks to do around the house. Most families are going to give their children some allowance, some spending money anyway. If your child needs extra money provide him a legitimate way of earning it rather than stealing it.

3. If you find things regularly missing and your child denies the theft you may want to try this: Don't query him. This only provokes denials and further lies. If you are pretty sure he did it, then have him pay it back, work it off, replace it, or make up for it. It is a matter of having him pay a consequence in the form of setting the record right. Adding extra punishment (restrictions) will not necessarily add to the lesson learned.

   Yes, you may be making a mistake by assuming he did it. But, better you err on this side for a change than let him get away with stealing. You can even say, "I may be wrong; maybe you didn't do it. If you didn't do it, I'm sorry, but you will still have to replace the money (or whatever is stolen)."

   By not asking him if he did it you prevent him from lying. It's pointless to set a trap for your child just so you can test out his honesty. Questioning him also gives him practice at lying. Some parents say that by having their child "own up" to a wrongdoing it will be better for the child than if he lies. Yet, by avoiding a confrontation of, "Did you do it?"

you can completely focus on the stealing, rather than the combination of theft plus lying.

"My child lies to me." As was mentioned above there are times when you can avoid setting a trap for a child to lie. But, there are many times when it cannot be avoided or when you would not anticipate a lie. In assessing the seriousness of lies you should take several factors into consideration:

1. The *frequency.* How long has the lying been going on? If lying is prolonged over a year's period it is more significant than an occasional spell of lying.

2. *Persistence.* Will your child readily confess after being confronted or will he persist at lying?

3. *Guilt.* Does he appear guilty after being caught in a lie? Crying, apologizing, showing fear or shame are all more positive indicators than the child showing anger or trying to talk his way out of it with excuses.

4. *Repentance.* A healthy sign is for children to want to make up or set things right after a lie. After the lie is discovered children who tend to be more compliant and agreeable are better off than those who are more defiant and resistant.

5. *Age.* The older the child, particularly a teen, the more serious the problem.

If your child has shown most all the danger indicators: frequent and persistent lying, not showing guilt, being more resistant after being caught, and being an older child, you have a much more difficult situation. You may want to seek professional help if the problem is severe. The techniques professionals use to work with very serious lying problems are the same ones that are dis-

134

cussed here, but the application of the techniques can be more demanding and may require close monitoring to be effective.

For parents facing the problem of their child lying the following ideas will guide you in combating the situation:

1. When you catch your child in a lie, do not press too strongly for "reasons" for the lie. Most children will not give you an adequate answer anyway. Go ahead and ask the "Why?" questions but ask it in a mild, nonjudgemental, nonthreatening fashion.

2. If you receive no adequate answer (a shrug of shoulders, "I don't know", or crying) *don't* get angry. Keep control over your temper even if you have to walk away. You probably will be frustrated but losing your temper will only compound the problem. If you regularly get very angry your child will make a strong attempt to cover a lie in order to escape your anger. Recall the technique of Saving Face. It may be better to avoid asking "Why?" questions, but don't avoid the issue.

3. Tell your child that you are deeply disappointed in him. Say it in a nonthreatening way, yet make it sound sincere. Your disapproval can be much more powerful than getting angry or yelling.

4. If no apology is immediately forthcoming then give him a short period of time to feel the guilt. Probably not less than ½ hour and not more than a day. Most children will respond to this period of withdrawal of attention by seeking you out and apologizing.

5. Don't blow the lie out of proportion. If the lie was covering some inappropriate act or avoiding a task

then you should focus on the target more than on the lie. If you focus too much attention on the lie the child has successfully shifted your attention away from the real target. He will learn that misbehavior can be hidden or screened by a lie. For this reason and because you want to *demonstrate* (not just verbally tell) that the lie was of no benefit, go back to focusing on the target or inappropriate behavior.

6. Focusing attention on the behavior gives your child the message that you want him to take responsibility for his actions which he tried to cover up by the lie. Review the section on Consequences in Chapter 2. If your child can *now* go back and do what he should have done in the first place, then have him do that. Try to avoid unnatural consequences and too harsh of punishments. Make the consequences follow in a logical connection with the original task.

7. A policy of having too harsh of consequence makes it more likely that the child will lie in the future. If there is already a very harsh punishment, adding a lie does not seem to the child to be incurring further harshness. After all, if he can get away with the lie he gets out of a lot of trouble. If he gets caught the added punishment for the lie doesn't seem that much worse than the original harsh consequence would have been.

8. Review your consistency on follow-through. If you tend to be lax and inconsistent in checking or enforcing rules it will be to the child's immediate advantage to "test" the system with a lie. It be-

comes a matter of percentages. A lie may work because you don't check. This builds a habit of lying because it pays off some of the time.

"They never want to stay home." This complaint hurts because parents feel rejected by their children. The child avoids being home and usually avoids talking with you. Why might this situation happen? There are several reasons for your child avoiding contacts with you.

1. The most obvious reason is that kids are doing something that is not approved of. Drinking, smoking, illegal drugs, sex, mischief, and hanging around with undesirable friends at unapproved places are the general fears. You can assess the extent of the problem by looking at several significant indicators. One indicator is school performance. Good school grades, a "C" or better average is a good sign, especially if there are no "D's" or "F's". Another indicator is the child's handling of chores. If your child usually completes chores without frequent reminders it is also a good sign. An obvious indicator is the amount of trouble the child has already gotten into. Has your child been in trouble at school or in the community? Finally, another indicator is the feedback you receive from neighbors and friends. Negative or even neutral feedback is a cause for concern.

Summarizing, if your child is getting poor grades, neglecting chores, has a history of trouble in school or with the law, and you have not received positive feedback from others about your child then indeed there is a major problem. With *all* of the negative indicators present you may want to seek professional help. Regardless, you may want to try techniques such as: firming up your Rules (review the section beginning on page 23 if needed), gradually add more work to the child's list, especially if he has few responsibilities, and consulting with teachers about what you can do to help bring up the grades.

2. Another reason for your children avoiding you is that you are not listening and understanding them. This situation happens when parents are not practicing Reflective Listening, but rather become judgemental. Imagine seeking a friend to talk with when that friend seems to only half listen, tells you want to do and think, disapproves of your way of handling any situation, shows no confidence in your judgement and is quick to point out your mistakes; you probably would not continue to seek out that friend's council. The same situation happens when parents try to control too much of the child's life. Parents think they know best (they usually do) and try to head-off future problems. Yet, this tactic deprives the child of the freedom to make his own mistakes. The dilemma is one of degree. Sure, it is important to exert some influence when the possible consequence is disaster, but there are many situations which, even if the wrong decision is made, would not lead to real disaster.

The teenage years are particularly vulnerable to the battle of parental guidance versus childhood independence. The best guidelines for you to follow is to learn Reflective Listening and practice it! You should reduce the number of rules you have to the minimum. However, those few rules should be rigidly enforced. Other situations should be a matter of negotiation rather than parental control. In this way it becomes advantageous for the child to negotiate with you. He can often get *some* of what he wants rather than a flat "no".

Matters such as religion and morality are sources of conflict. When you try to verbally force your religion and morality upon your youngster it can be a real battle. Morality is picked up from watching and living within a family. Morality is not so much taught as absorbed. This absorption of morality takes place in the early years of childhood. By the teen years it is well entrenched — whatever the type of morality. Altering or modifying a teen's morality by direct instruction is near impossible. The process only serves to alienate children.

3. Some good things to practice are Reflective Listening, allowing your child to talk at least half the time, showing interest in his activities (not to be overdone), and allowing more use of natural consequences rather than parental authority. Again, keep the number of rules to a minimum and avoid harsh punishment.

Bad Attitude

Concerns over children's attitude form a strong group of concerns. Here are some typical complaints:

"I can't stand his bad attitude."

"She argues constantly."

"I can't stand the crying and whining."
"He's afraid to leave my side."
"She's shy."
"My child is afraid of ____."
"My child is afraid to be by himself."
In order to change and prevent attitudinal problems let's examine each complaint in detail.

"I can't stand his bad attitude." What exactly is attitude? You can see it in a facial expression, tone of voice, words, and actions. Most often, bad attitude is a sign of defiance or anger following your request, command or question. An old-fashioned method of correcting "bad" attitude was to be knocked on your ear (to put it mildly). Most modern child psychologists would frown on that technique. Times have changed. They would argue for another solution, one which is less direct but perhaps more powerful and lasting.

Let me say that I believe that the old-fashioned (sometimes brutal) slap, spanking or other physical punishment often *did* work. It worked for centuries and still will work. So, why do many learned professionals discourage corporal punishment? There are at least four major reasons: first, many parents are inconsistent in the use of corporal punishment. Second, parents may postpone physical punishment until father comes home or until the issue is talked to death. Thirdly, there are other less severe methods which work. And fourthly, harsh punishment can engender tremendous fear in kids. This fear can be disabling and often lasts a lifetime. Sociologists might add a fifth reason for discouraging corporal punishment. Due to the effects of modeling, one generation will pass on a tendency toward violence to the next generation.

Typical Parent Complaints: What do I do now?

If the above arguments will not persuade you to abstain from corporal punishment think about the following suggestions which will make corporal punishment more effective:

1. If there is something about your child's "attitude" that is intolerable do something *immediately*. Do not wait for words, threats, father, or Santa Claus. Immediate consequences are likely to be most effective. Immediate means immediate, instantaneous, or quicker.

2. The sooner you catch the unacceptable behavior the calmer you will be and the less likely you will be to completely lose your temper. Also, the milder the punishment will be. Waiting until things get out of hand is unwise. Do something at the very *first sign* of unacceptable behavior.

3. Be extremely consistent in supplying a consequence. If you act like a "slot machine" and the youngster doesn't know whether to expect a swift punishment or be excused, he will "play" you. If a child *knows* what will happen he will be less likely to pull your lever.

4. If your child consistently tests you, if he frequently demonstrates unacceptable behavior, you are not following one of the above three points closely enough.

As I told you earlier, there are techniques other than corporal punishment to deal with poor attitude. One method is to make a distinction between the behavior you are requesting and your child's attitude. The requested or *target* behavior is the task the child must complete. What did you want the child to do? His attitude is a separate

141

dimension which shows how he feels about the task or about you. This distinction dictates that the target behavior be enforced while the child's attitude is ignored. You should not call him back or interrupt him from completing the job in order to call attention to his bad attitude (mumbling, saying a "smart" remark, saying, "I won't" or slamming the door). If you consistently ignore the bad attitude, but strictly enforce completion of the target the poor attitude will gradually fade away.

Bad attitude is an attention-getting device which will tend to disappear if not rewarded with attention (even negative attention). Ignoring may mean sending him to his room or outside after the task is finished, walking away yourself, plugging your ears and/or biting your tongue. For how long? A child has difficulty with being ignored even for five minutes. But, be prepared to ignore your tantrum-throwing child for hours. Rewarding tantrums or bad attitude with your positive *or* negative attention is not what you want to do. Wait until the inappropriate behavior stops. Your child needs your attention and assistance more than you need his. He will need to drop the bad attitude in order to have you pay attention to him. As with all other techniques there is a critical need here to be consistent with your ignoring. The child will learn that it is not to his advantage to have a bad attitude and he will change if you are consistent.

Here is another technique which I have sometimes found to be helpful when other ideas have failed. If your child has a minimum of chores or responsibilities and maintains a consistently bad attitude consider this: assign a minimum of two good hours of work per day, every day. The work can be tough jobs around the house (e.g., waxing floors, cleaning ovens, washing walls, etc.). Make sure that he sticks with the task(s) until completion. He may waste time, but if you start early, after school or in the morning on weekends, the task(s) will consume entire evenings and large parts of days. Allow the child to complain freely. Don't allow play until the jobs are completed. Stick with this policy for at least a month. I could offer several possible explanations for the technique working and even a few which might suggest that it should not work. All I can say is that some parents who complain that their teenage child has attitude problems (often surrounding arguments over freedom and restrictions) benefit from this technique when other ideas have failed. It may be that the child initally has a poor self-concept, partially because he lacks the esteem-building of accomplishment. By providing (forcing) lots of opportunities for accomplishments the child will develop a more positive self-concept.

"She argues constantly." Many of the same devices used in "attitude" problems are pertinent here. Children argue when they wish to postpone or avoid a chore or instruction. When you try to "limit" what your child thinks are freedoms, things which he feels he has a "right to", this also triggers arguments. Here are several things to consider:

1. Don't argue back or yell.
2. Don't repeat yourself.
3. Do ignore further pleas or arguments.
4. Do ignore continued "Why?" questions.
5. If the child is instructed to do something see that it is done. Give him a reasonable time limit to comply. Leaving the immediate area helps allow the

child to save face. He will tend to do the task when you are not watching.
6. Stop giving preventative warnings. This means stop telling your child what to avoid "or they will get into trouble". Avoid these statements: "Don't stay out too late." "Don't drive too fast." "Be careful." "Don't get into any trouble." "Did you remember to ____?" "Did you forget to ____?" "Don't you think you should ____?"

"I can't stand the crying and whining." Whining is an attention-getting mechanism. A child can use it when he doesn't want to do something or when he's forced to stop doing something. Whining and whimpering can be maintained for long durations and are very annoying. This is a device a child uses as a protest. Here are various points to consider when trying to eliminate whining:
1. Have you given your child an "adequate" amount of attention? If you are not sure, give a significantly greater amount of attention to your child for several weeks and see if it reduces the whining. Attention means 100% focus of attention on the child even if it's for short periods of time. Divided attention is *not* good enough. Make sure your attention is given at another time than during or immediately after whining. You can understand that attention is rewarding and you don't want to reward whining.
2. Since whining is an inappropriate attention-getter an effective treatment is to frustrate the child's efforts. Ignore whining. You will need to do it consistently. Make sure you endure (ignore) longer than your child persists. When the child's whine is

not reinforced by your attention, positive or negative, he will *gradually* turn to other techniques to get your attention.

3. Reinforce appropriate attention-getting. For example, when your child becomes quiet or when he is doing something that is acceptable you may then offer your attention. In this way you are teaching him how to get your attention in a more agreeable fashion.

4. Crying is handled in the same way as whining. Crying can either be attention-getting or a device to manipulate you. If crying is chronic it can be modified by ignoring, while still paying attention to acceptable behavior. If no attention follows the crying it will stop.

"He's afraid to leave my side." There is a basic dependence and clinginess which is normal in very young children. When should this need to hang on to you give way? By two or three years of age there should be clear signs of straying. By this I mean your child should be content to play with other children in your absence. He should stop following you around, constantly. One of the major reasons for children keeping close is that it satisfies the parent. A clinging child often has a parent who wants the child to cling. So, you need to examine your needs to see if you are unknowingly encouraging this behavior. Here are several items to consider:

1. Find ways to separate yourself from your child. This can be done gradually by having him play in one room and you go to another for increasingly longer stays. You may even need to retreat to *your* bedroom to separate yourself. Start with the door

open and with subsequent stays, shut the door, in stages.

2. Leave the child in the care of others for increasingly long stays. You need to leave despite the child's tears and pleading. A gradual transition can be made by having a babysitter come to your home. Progress by leaving the child at other people's homes.

3. If you are rather preoccupied with your child you will need to develop other interests. This will necessitate that you learn to ignore the child for longer periods of time. By making sure there are other available people (or peers) to provide the needed attention you can socially wean him.

"She's shy." This observation is identical in nature to the above problem. Follow the above suggestions ("He's afraid to leave my side.") for ideas to use on shyness.

"My child is afraid of _____." Fears are normal and common. The world can be a frightening place filled with storms, demons, darkness, animals, and the unknown. Many childhood fears seem to peak, then die a natural death. Lightning doesn't strike, the dog doesn't bite, and the ghost didn't attack from the closet. Yet, some fears persist throughout adulthood. Here are several ideas to consider about fears:

1. Children acquire fears by imitating parental fears. A mother who holds her daughter tight during a lightning storm may be teaching the child to be fearful. A child who "needs" a light on may have a parent who fears the dark or feared it as a child. One first step in preventing a fear is to avoid modeling fearful behavior.

2. Once acquired, a fear is not easily talked away. Rather than expend energy talking kids out of fears it is better to assume an expectation that suggests the fear is not terribly important. This can be done by listening to the child's fear story once. You may even be persuaded to open the closet door, or whatever, the first time. But don't expect that will cure the fear. The second time the same fear appears you can reflect back to the child that your understand he is frightened. Avoid spending time arguing him out of it. Stay calm yourself, smile understandingly at the fear, and then leave. Don't pay a great deal of attention to the fear. Recall that attention has a tendency to reinforce things and cause them to persist.

3. Most fears can be eliminated by one of two methods, either gradual or abrupt exposure. The gradual exposure method can be explained using the following example: Many "night-time" fears have been relieved by leaving a light on or a door open. Rather than overcoming the fear this practice can enhance the fear. If the lights go off either because of a bulb burning out or a power failure you have an immediate panic. A gradual exposure remedy would begin by closing the door over a period of weeks in graded steps. You and the child plan together when and how much to close the door with the eventual goal of the door fully closed at night. Most children will participate in the plan if they feel that they have some say in how much the door is shut. If you receive no cooperation you should go ahead with the plan, making sure the child knows

147

each step. There is no rush so you can go slow.

The same program works well with a light on at night. Begin by switching to a smaller bulb. Continue by shading the bulb until it's dark in the room. You can go as fast or slow in the process as you see fit. Most children who reach the goal are delighted and confident in their new found abilities or bravery.

An abrupt exposure procedure, as might be expected, is for the door to be closed or the light off on the first night. This process is initally more fearful. A comparison with the gradual exposure process is difficult. We have little firm information to judge from. The abrupt procedure does work, perhaps more rapidly than the gradual method. Howerver, many people prefer the gradual method because they feel it is less painful and more humane. The parent is free to choose the approach which most suits the problem. The above procedures can easily be applied to fear of animals or other objects.

4. As you may have guessed, the author is not in favor of living with or appeasing childhood fears. Fears can be much more easily overcome when young. If appeased, fears have a tendency to stock and sometimes grow.

Not all of my colleagues agree with the notion of forcing a confrontation — even a gradual one. Here is a dialogue I might have with a colleague on the issue:

Colleague: I once counseled a young girl as a result of her strong fear over a particular, rather dark and forboding, painting. The parents were well educated and bought an expensive painting from a friend. I suggested that the painting be removed. This relieved the girl's fear. I instructed the parents to tell her that they liked the painting very much and would wait until she felt comfortable enough to obtain the painting back.

Author: Where was the painting stored?
Colleague: The painting was hung in a friend's home. The couple visited these friends frequently and had a playmate for the girl.
Author: What happened?
Colleague: In about four months the girl spontaneously announced that it would be OK to take the painting home. She was no longer afraid of it.
Author: The girl was exposed to the painting at the friend's home. That is why she extinguished her fear.
Colleague: Other examples I can give you show that no exposure is necessary for some fears to go away.
Author: With your method it may be that the child doesn't outgrow the fear. The feared object may be forced to be banned indefinitely, perhaps at an inconvenience to parents. Besides, forced exposure does not always mean there will be adverse effects. Gradual exposure has not been shown to be harmful.
Colleague: Nevertheless, my method has worked and is effective in some situations.

The reader will need to judge for himself. I am still firmly convinced that fears can be overcome rapidly and effectively.

5. Regardless of technique, fears have a tendency to spontaneously reappear. Some remnant remains with the possibility that the fear may emerge after

a prolonged absence. Expect the reappearance. Usually the reappearance is transitory and will disappear abruptly. If not, then simply reinstitute the original procedure.

6. Sometimes fears cannot be easily introduced. For example, a child may develop a fear of flying or become afraid to go on a long trip. When gradual exposure is desired but difficult to present in real life the process can be accomplished in imagery. You can take your child on an imaginary trip and gradually introduce the feared situation. Make a game of it. By repeatedly introducing the frightening thing or situation in imagery the child will be less frightened.

"My child is afraid to be by himself." This is a common fear and may be treated using the technique outlined above. It is listed separately because it is so common and can lead to major problems in adult life.

Some people marry, remain together, seek unhappy friendships and are utterly miserable because they could not tolerate being alone. You are encouragaed to allow your children to be alone, regularly. The process can be gradual and may start when the child is a toddler. When your child is occupied, leave for a brief time. When done slowly the child will become accustomed to your absence and will feel confident that you will return. By beginning when the child is young you can continue and build upon the process over many years. Increasingly longer absences still find your child making use of these periods rather than having him desperately waiting for your return.

Here are some suggestions to follow if your child has a fear of being alone:

1. Begin by arranging something interesting for your child to do. Leave for a short time (the duration depends upon age; between five and twenty minutes). When you return be enthusiastic. Praise your child for being good. Heap on attention. Repeat the process at random times over a period of months. The idea is that your child will be content with being alone because he will get lots of attention *later*. You will find that he becomes less desperate during your absences. The intrinsic interest in the activity will also help to override your absence.
2. It may be necessary to help structure the periods of being alone. That is, you will want to prevent bad feelings by having fun things to do in the interim until your return.
3. Expand the periods of absence. Provide less structure as time goes on. You are introducing increased frustration. The child will need to become industrious in order to entertain himself.

Miscellaneous issues

In this section we cover a group of rather unrelated problems they are:

Bedwetting is a problem.

"I'm concerned about her nightmares."

"We differ on our discipline." Parental conflict.

"What do I say when he/she says,

    'I hate you.'

    'You don't love me.'

    'I want to go with daddy/mommy (the absent parent).'

'The divorce is your fault.'

Each one of these topics are now reviewed with numerous suggestions you may want to try.

Bedwetting is a problem. There are several techniques that can be used to deal with enuresis or bedwetting. The trend has been to avoid teasing or hollering at a bedwetter. This trend is certainly more humane not to mention that the teasing and hollering are not effective in keeping bedsheets dry.

1. Make bedwetting the child's responsibility. Removing wet bedclothes and bedsheets should be the province of the youngster. The soiled articles can be put in water if the child is very young or washed by hand or machine for children old enough to accomplish the task. Remaking the bed with clean sheets is also part of taking on the responsibility.

2. By having the child assume the burdens of stripping, cleaning, and remaking the bed it relieves your burden, making the entire situation less unpleasant for everyone. Children will readily take this responsibility on to ward off the normal feelings of guilt and shame. Since the burden is squarely on the child there is a natural desire to cease bedwetting and avoid the extra work.

3. Restricting water consumption in the evening may make it easier to learn bladder control, but it does not stop bedwetting. The only thing people report about restricting water consumption is that there is less of a puddle.

4. I am not enthusiastic about regularly waking children in the middle of the night to have them relieve

themselves. While waking a child during his sleep may have merit, especially when you expand the duration that control can be sustained, it has drawbacks. Chief among the drawbacks is that it is a burden on parents. If all other approaches fail and you are willing to miss a little sleep then give it a try.

5. A popular technique to encourage bladder control is to provide incentives (rewards) for a dry bed. Incentives can be a star or check on a display chart. It can be earning points toward something. Have your child help with or entirely make a chart to be posted. On wet days there is no reward. The child cleans up after himself. On dry days there is the incentive and even a parental congratulations. The trick to the procedure is to make the incentive strong enough or fun enough for the child to keep trying to acquire regular bladder control. The good thing about stars, checks, or points is that is not an all-or-nothing system. There is value in remaining dry even if it is not on consecutive nights. Any day the bed is dry contributes toward the goal.

6. There is a mechanical device, often sold through catalogue stores, that rings a bell or buzzer when the child begins to wet. The device is a pad the child sleeps on. When the pad becomes wet it trips a circuit which engages a buzzer to wake the child. These devices have various claims of effectiveness. The devices work with some children and could be used if other techniques fail.

7. I neglected to mention possible physical reasons for bedwetting. There are physical as well as psycho-

logical and developmental reasons for bedwetting. It is always a safe bet to eliminate possible physical problems. However, my guess is that there are statistically more emotional and developmental issues that contribute to bedwetting than purely physical problems. Bladder control is a difficult skill to learn. It has a very broad range for what constitutes the normal or average period for mastery. Bedwetters tend to exhibit sporadic control and sometimes can remain dry when visiting a relative or living with someone else for a short time. Other bedwetters have never been "dry" and are somewhat more difficult to teach.

8. A strategy which many counselors follow is when working with multi-problem families, there is an enuretic problem, they tend to work on the other problems first. When family life becomes stable and pleasant, parents often report that bedwetting has ceased.

"I'm concerned about her nightmares." Bad dreams or nightmares are almost universal. Nearly every child has occasional nightmares. But what about the child who has nightmares every night? She may awake in a sweat and let out a frightful scream. She may come into your room and want to crawl into your bed. In spite of all the talk about dreams, the work of Freud, and laboratory research there is a lot we don't know about dreams. If your child has persistent nightmares you probably have already tried reassurance, scolding, comforting, logic, and almost every other remedy. What happens when these devices fail?

The oldest boy, four years of age, had been having

"night terrors" for about six months. These episodes became daily occurrences. The parents were very worried. The parents had been in the habit of taking turns getting up in the middle of the night with Robbie. They went into Robbie's room, briefly talked with him, reassured him that everything was all right, hugged or held him and then tucked him back into bed.

Regardless of what initially triggered the nightmares the present pattern was being reinforced by large doses of love and attention. Look for reasons why behaviors persist. Rather than beginning with mysterious, symbolic, or complex causative factors, look for the immediate variables, in this case parental attention, surrounding the behavior, nightmares. The suggestion was that one or both parents initially give Robbie attention when tucking him in. The attention could be reading to him, playing a short game, or talking with him. A hug and kiss won't hurt either. When the nightmare came, the parents were instructed to stay in their bed regardless of the boy's screams. Actually, parents were allowed to quietly sneak up to the boy's door and listen if they felt the need to check things out. Nevertheless, there was to be no attention given until the morning.

The first thing you might expect was that it was difficult for the parents to refrain from comforting the boy. They were afraid something would happen to him if they didn't check on him. It was in the second week that the parents did carry out the instructions completely. They returned after that week and related their initial skepticism. The couple was almost ready to give up this "torture" when suddenly Robbie slept one night without screaming. Neither parent was able to determine exactly if the boy had a nightmare or not. But, at least he didn't scream. Robbie seldom remembered being awakened by a nightmare or having his parents come in or even his screams. Therefore, it was impossible for him to reliably report what happened, besides he was four years old. In the fourth week he had cried loudly only twice. At the six month follow-up the parents reported that Robbie screamed only once in the previous month. The boy stopped mentioning anything about dreams. When the parents stayed up late they could not hear any signs of nightmares. It appeared that by withdrawing the ongoing support (parental attention) it eliminated the problem.

The idea that we can alter our behavior by forcing ourselves to imagine success has been around for years. There was the "power of positive thinking" craze and the slogan, "every day and in every way I'm getting better and better", which people repeated endlessly to themselves. Shakespeare's "assume the virtue" concept and modern athletics use of "imagining success" are all identifying a tool which can help to alter ourselves.

There is some evidence in the psychological literature that the technique of imagery can be effectively used against nightmares. After talking with your child about her nightmares try identifying repetitive elements. For example, a common element may be a particularly frightening figure or animal, a chase scene, a scary place or being hurt. You then instruct your child on how to respond (in the dream) to this condition. Some ways the child can "respond" is by taking the mask off of the frightening figure, by leading the animal into a cage and shutting the door, by stopping the chase and inviting the "thing" to have ice cream with you, by turning the lights on in the scary place and find out that the child is in a friendly place, or by discovering that the knife is made of butterscotch and tastes good. The child can rehearse the new response in imagery or you can instruct her to use it whenever the next nightmare happens. Try to convice her that simply by trying out this new idea the scary dream will end happily. Each night before bedtime remind her to use the new plan.

"We differ on our discipline." Parental conflict. Arguments over child-rearing can become destructive, with both sides locked in combat. Factors such as favoritism, jealousy, leniency, and strictness enter into parental conflict. If you argue frequently and intensely over discipline here are some suggestions:

1. Seek out and agree to follow a guide such as this book, another book, or a child-rearing class. Both partners need to read, study, or attend classes together.

2. Don't argue about discipline at the same time you argue about other matters. If you argue about the kids you should not drift to other conflicts.

3. You may want to start out with a clean slate — no rules or chores for the kids. Then begin adding only those rules, chores, or permissive allowances that both parents agree to. If there is disagreement on any issue then skip it and work on another issue. Post the agreed-upon issues with both sides signing the list. Don't do anything about those issues which no agreement has been reached. This might sound like you are ignoring conflicts. Actually, it forces both sides to negotiate, compromise, and feel an equal partner in the decisions.

157

4. If your partner is resistant to the above suggestions attempt to enlist his/her support for obtaining counseling. If the spouse flatly refuses to participate in counseling with you try this: Take control over what you can control. For example, you have control over your time. Use your time, energy and support as reinforcers for the kids. If you are consistently following the principles discussed in this book, even without your spouse's support, you can accomplish many objectives.

5. If the kids are bothering one parent then basically it is that parent's responsibility to take whatever action is necessary. Avoid being caught between your spouse, who expects you to solve all the problems, and your child who feels that your spouse is unfair or too strict. Stop being a mediator, peacemaker, arbitrator, or tension reducer. Keeping peace in the family at all costs is a poor goal. If forced to confront each other, your spouse and children, they will usually work most things out by themselves. Your interference might even slow down the process.

6. If you find that the kids mind your spouse but not yourself then determine if you rely too heavily on your spouse to provide the discipline. Children will tend to ignore you if *you* don't enforce the rules. Children will also ignore you if you hestitate, waiver, and make empty threats.

The wife who stays home all day, says "no" too often, gets frustrated, yells, doesn't follow through, and finds herself ignored by the kids may grow to resent the children, resent her husband who maintains control, and feel like a failure. She must learn to begin taking control by setting up situations over which she *does* have control and which she *can* follow through. The husband who works all day, comes home to his hot meal, newspaper, TV and selfish diversions, and who expects his wife to raise the kids will find that the only way he can maintain control is either by giving his wife orders or by resorting to harsh punishment. His wife needs to say "no" to his orders for the children. If that sounds like I am promoting parental conflict perhaps it's true in this instance. Who said the task of child-rearing was easy or without conflict? If the conflict is between parents that's where it needs to be resolved, not with kids caught in the middle.

"What do I say when he/she says,

'I hate you!' Some answers which would fit, depending upon the specific situation are: "I know you're angry at me for not letting you go to the movies." "I know you are very upset with me." "What you are feeling is that I'm not being fair with you." Other responses are ignoring the child and enforcing the rule you set up by following through with consequences. The above responses were examples of Reflective Listening, Ignoring, and Consequences which are presented in Chapter 2. Review these techniques if you are not sure when and how to use each.

'You don't love me!' As in the previous example you would want to use one of the three techniques mentioned. Don't assume here or in the above example that your child necessarily means what he is saying. Both exclamations, "I hate you!" and "You don't love me!" mean an expression of anger, which may quickly pass or it may be a manipula-

tive device to avoid doing a chore. Understand why these exclamations are being said rather than overreact to them.

'I want to go with daddy/mommy (the absent parent).' Here again practice Reflective Listening. Most likely, the child is upset with some immediate issue. A young child often uses this when he is frustrated and wants to get back at you. You might say, "I know you don't want to clean your room; your father/mother doesn't make you do these things." Avoid getting very angry at your child's rejection of you. Stick to the task at hand and make sure he does the assigned chore, *now.*

'The divorce is your fault!' A young child or even a teen needs to blame someone for his unhappiness. This may be an attempt to force you into returning to your ex-spouse. It also may be an expression of anger in the hopes that you will modify the existing chores or rules.

Regardless of the reason, it is a good oportunity to use Reflective Listening. You can listen and understand, yet need not change what you are doing. Don't let the child set a hook into your guilt with the result being that you ease off. Sometimes children can be cruel without fully understanding or even caring how deeply you are hurting. All they may know is whether they were successful or not in getting what they wanted. If the child is not successful he will stop sticking the knife in and try some other tactic.

Divorced parents can be an easy mark for a pushy child. Parents want to "make up" for the divorce. Compensating for the divorce results in letting a child get away with things he would not otherwise be allowed to get away with. Unfortunately, easing off is definitely not the way to reduce the child's or your distress. Children need stability and look to you to provide that stability. By continuing the same firm rules you will be providing that stability. Your child can *trust* in your consistency. The child's world is altered enough by the divorce without the added turmoil of your inconsistency and lack of structure.

CHAPTER 6
PATTERNS

Psychology, with one of its goals being the prediction and control of behavior, is largely based on identifying consistent patterns. The best guess for what will happen in the future is a repetition of what happened in the past. Thus, identifying life themes, scripts, personality traits, or habits is extremely important. And fortunately there are things about children that are consistent and predictable.

There are many isolated actions, rare behaviors, or occasional actions your child will exhibit. Making sense of these unusual (not typical) behaviors and trying to encourage or discourage these rare acts is very difficult. Examples of rare events might be stealing from a store, ditching a class, deliberately breaking a toy, leaving without telling you the destination, and sexual activity. If these examples happen infrequently it will be hard to do anything about them *directly*. Sure, you can punish. But, because the acts happen only once in a great while (and repetition is the key to teaching or learning) there is much less surety in your child learning from the punishment. The method advocated is to tackle your child's normal, regular patterns. If the child's general pattern of behavior is acceptable you should not have any great difficulty with these unusual situations.

Some patterns of behavior are more important than others. Which shoe is put on first is an unimportant pattern. Yet, there are many patterns that are meaningful. Below are some popularly discussed patterns of behavior:

inadequacy	shy	attention-seeking
inferiority	jealousy	authoritarian
guilty	insecurity	superiority
fearful	helplessness	defensiveness

Actually, we infer one of those pattern tendencies from what we observe. You can't peek into someone's mind and look directly at a shyness or defensiveness center. You observe the person's behavior and look for a consistent pattern. You *infer* from a set of behaviors the internal patten which is labeled shyness or defensiveness. When you "know" or "understand" someone, what you are saying is that you can identify some of that person's patterns.

Look for patterns in your child's behavior. What does your child *usually* do? Let's say that you've noticed that your child ignores your instructions. Begin by examining the usual pattern. You might have asked him to clean up a small mess. Your request triggered the customary ignoring response "ya" or "OK, in a minute." Your child's verbal response was followed by inactivity.

You might discover that in a large percentage of these situations you forget about the request, ultimately cleaning the mess yourself. You might give several reminders. Occasionally you explode with anger, perhaps a spanking. By focusing on patterns you discover that your child didn't *usually* clean up the mess with or without the spanking. You cleaned it up! No wonder he has learned to ignore you. That ignoring habit will probably expand to include teachers and other authority figures. If the pattern continues into adulthood what would you guess the employee-employer relationship to be like? What might you expect to happen when his wife talks to him?

The Struggle to Overcome Childhood

Adults' major sources of conflict are rooted in childhood. During childhood your principal needs and desires take shape. No single event is strong enough to form these primary life themes; they develop over years of learning. Here are born the principal fears, passions, and strivings of your life. Examples of such themes are:

I'm afraid to be alone.
I like nice things.
I must be a success.
I need to be considered smart or important.
I need to please father or mother.
I like peace and quiet.
I'm going to raise my kids differently than I was raised.
I can do anything.
There's something wrong with me.
I have to be liked by everyone.

Everyone is out to take advantage of me.
I have to prove myself.
I want to be heard.
If you really knew me, you wouldn't like me.
I'm a failure.
I don't like to work.
My family is important.
I'm unloveable.
I must have nothing but the best.

With effort and perhaps some assistance most people can identify six or more themes which dictate many aspects of their lives. These themes are guiding forces that we learn in childhood; they generally remain fixed throughout our lives. Some themes lead to satisfaction and success while others guide us into misery and failure.

Conflict arises from contradictions in our themes (internal) or between our themes and the outside environment (external). An example of an internal conflict is feeling a need to be liked yet feeling that if someone gets close they won't like me. Another common example is liking nice things but not liking to work. Remember I mean overriding life themes, ones that stay with you and are the unspoken drives behind your decisions. Yes, most of us like nice things, but for some it can determine where they live, who they marry, the type of friends they make, the places they go, and people they meet. External contradictions can take many forms. You can have a handicap, thus preventing or reducing the fulfillment of a life goal. Factors such as having children, incurring debts, lacking education or training, and bad luck may frustrate certain of your life

168

themes.

During child rearing you will confront conflicts among your own life themes. For example, you may feel that you want your daughter to be free of the oppressive sternness of parental authority yet you also want to feel very much in control. Another example is wanting your children to be mature yet not wanting them to make mistakes. These parental urges and goals are formed through our early family experiences. Other common conflicts are: I want to be important in this family (have the family depend on me) yet I don't like to be stifled by everyone coming to me when they have problems. I'm afraid to be alone yet I want my kids to go off and play with their peers.

The following short case history on Jamie illustrates how an early experience pattern for the mother resulted in adopting a faulty child-rearing policy.

Jamie is eleven years old. His mother has been married for two years to her third husband. Jamie's father died shortly after Jamie's nine-year-old brother was born. Jamie remembers George, his first step-father. He also faintly remembers George beating up his mother. Jamie's mother and current step-father appear happy and the family, including two older step brothers is tranquil — except for Jamie.

Ruth complains that Jamie is restless, moody, and forgetful. Ruth admits she has a short temper, but feels she has been too permissive in the past. "I guess I spoiled him by giving him all my love and attention when he was young." This was not the first time Jamie was brought into a counseling center. Several times in the past he was sent to a counselor.

Usually only Jamie was seen, in play therapy, the counselor called it. Ruth felt the boy had benefited from the play therapy. But, the problem she had with him didn't change. Now even his teachers were complaining about his lack of attention and isolation (from peers). After several sessions with the family and several sessions with Jamie alone it was evident what the trouble was. Jamie didn't hear Ruth's requests, instructions, and yelling. He learned that if he pretended not to hear her original request he could sometimes avoid doing chores. Most children can tell when mother means business and when she is just throwing a temper tantrum.

Repeatedly during family counseling Ruth would turn to Jamie and say, "See what he (the counselor) is saying; if you don't put your toys away the first time then you'll be in trouble. There won't be a next time." Each time the counselor reminded her that she was warning the boy by these threats. She agreed but defended herself by saying she just wanted to make sure that Jamie understood.

"Yes, Ruth," the counselor said, "but he will learn to understand by what you *do*, not what you say." Unlike other parents Ruth was not able to act. Why? Ruth revealed that her own father said things only once and she was very afraid of him. She promised herself that she was not going to be that harsh on her children. Despite the counselor's efforts at establishing positive rewards for complying with parental requests, Ruth was unable to withhold the rewards when Jamie didn't do the work.

At this point the focus of counseling changed from Jamie to Ruth, where it really belonged. By freeing herself from the bonds of her childhood memories it enabled her to be more firm with her son. She gradually reconciled the idea of being firm while retaining and showing love. She saw how her step-father, although firm, was not loving. This enabled her to be more consistent at following through with her requests without the fear that Jamie would not love her.

What themes can you identify for Ruth and for Jamie?

Ruth: If I am harsh (strict or firm) then my son will be afraid of me. Talking is much less offensive than actions. Speaking-up only results in more conflicts. I want my son to like me. Being firm means unloving.

Jamie: Don't listen to people; they never mean (act) what they say. Protesting pays off. I don't respect people who are pushovers like my mother.

Can you see how Jamie's themes conflict with Ruth's? Can you also see how Ruth puts up with Jamie's insults and how Jamie continues to be insulting? What type of relationship might you guess Ruth has with her husband? Her employer? When Jamie marries and his wife wants to talk with him about some conflict what will his reaction be? If Jamie's wife tries to please him how much respect will he have toward her?

These questions may lead to accurate predictions. In that case you can feel good about your understanding of the person. You are better prepared for the likely outcomes. And, more importantly for child-rearing, you can alter your behavior in order to avoid faulty patterns or enhance desired patterns. If the predictions are not accurate then you need to study the patterns further.

People are often unaware of what is really driving or motivating them. The reason for self-exploration is that we model our main themes. Children have a strong tendency to imitate those themes. A course in "self analysis" is beyond the scope of this book. But if you are attempting to be the best parent possible you should work on discovering your life themes.

Whenever you encounter a situation that powerfully moves you, whether that feeling is anger, fear, love or disappointment, you might look for the roots in your own childhood. There is a story behind "just feeling that way," "having a hunch", or being unable to logically explain your feeling or decision. There is a logic and a pattern to that "illogical" feeling which is hidden by the years and by various experiences. It becomes a fascinating quest to trace the roots of intense feelings and illogical feelings. By discovering these roots, the patterns and major themes which fuel your decisions and actions, you can begin to free yourself from overreacting. You can deal with the present separately from the bondage of past experiences. This is one way to begin overcoming your childhood handicaps. Good luck in your quest!

Dependence Models

In times past it was safer to rely on others for happiness and security. In the less mobile cultures of yesterday you could rely on the family as an enduring support system. Religion also tended to be a firmer, static support. The key to our modern culture is change. Change provides us with less enduring external supports. Consequently, there is a greater need to build security within oneself. If you depend upon current life supports, with those supports being fluid and changeable, you are more vulnerable than in bygone days. Depending upon people is much riskier because times and people are more changeable. While there is a greater need to be internally secure there is the contradictory societal demand to relate to others, to get along with people. Being an island unto oneself is discouraged. We have a dilemma of contrasts. Being able to be reasonably content with isolation is countered by a striving toward and contentment with social interaction. No wonder life is so complicated.

There is a strong push for individuals to be self reliant and independent. People need to cope with these complexities. One simplified way to view the need for independence is by access to enjoyment. Dependence is described by the following figure:

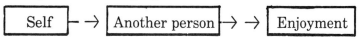

The dependent person relies on someone to obtain enjoyment. When that person is absent, enjoyment is blocked. Examples of this include the housewife who can only go out for a good time with her husband. The lonely housewife sits home. She hopes her mate will feel like going out when he comes home. Or, the husband who relies on his wife to arrange all the social appointments. If she is occupied, the husband's social plans are blocked.

The figure below demonstrates an independent relationship:

Self ⊢→ → → → → → → Enjoyment

Others ⊢ → → → → → → Enjoyment

Each person is able to have fun without "needing" someone else's help.

A contributing relationship is where both parties can reach the goal without the necessary support of the other but where each may enjoy extra enjoyment from the contribution of others.

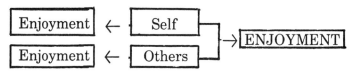

Having someone else present is not necessary yet the person's presence adds to the enjoyment. Some people are fooled into believing they have a contributory relationship when in fact they have a dependent relationship. One signpost of a contributory model is that you can find entertainment with or without your spouse. If the spouse chooses to join in, it will enhance the pleasure. If your spouse doesn't join in or doesn't choose to "go" and consequently you always decline an invitation then you may have a dependent relationship rather than a contributory model.

What counts, of course, is the *customary* behavior. A couple using the dependency or independent model as the prodominant pattern might have a potential problem. If the spouse dies, is unavailable, is a stick-in-the-mud, or doesn't enjoy activities you prefer, then you suffer under the dependency model. Likewise, if the independent model were exclusively the model of choice then there may be less commitment, courtesy, and trust present in the marriage.

These simplified models are just that — simplified. Yet they do provide guides to the meaning of independence and dependence. Parents model various forms of dependence and children usually imitate the behavior. Examine your pattern and determine if it is what you want to model for your children.

Reservoirs of Hostility

Many of us have a reservoir of bad feelings. For some people the reservoir is relatively small. If the storage is small, getting out the bad feelings seem to nearly drain the supply. But, there are others for which tapping off some of the bad feelings doesn't deplete the vast reserve.

A reservoir of bad feelings can be fed in many ways. Feeder streams build up the supply. We can name these feeder streams:

rejection	failure	dependency
unfairness	inconsistency	

You may be able to add to the above list. Healthy, well-adjusted people also have these feeder streams. The well-adjusted find good drainage systems and/or the inflow is relatively light. That is, there is either less reason to build up hostility or if hostility starts building, ways are found to "get it off one's chest". For others the streams either build too fast or there are fewer ways to rid themselves of these bad feelings.

When the reservoir, whether it contains a large or small supply of bad feelings, gets full, watch out. The reservoir can "overflow" in several ways. One way overflow is evident is when a person becomes overly angry. An explosion of temper can be reached by storing up feelings or "gunny sacking." Those problems flow into the reservoir until there's too much pressure. The dam breaks and tempers flair. Another sign of overflow is when a person rejects another's ideas or suggestions before really hearing them. Demonstrating impatience is a variation of showing an overflow of bad feelings. A subtle form of overflow is the "passive-aggressive" style. The person gets out anger (the aggressive part) by indirect (passive) methods. Forgetting, misplacing, accidents, and mistakes can all be ways of frustrating another person. Frustrating someone by indirect means helps reduce the reservoir of anger without directly showing anger. The "passive-ag-

175

gressive" style is a favorite of children who are not allowed to get directly angry at parents.

As adults you can start to deal with the backlog of bad feelings by recognizing when you are overreacting to the immediate situation. It is a good idea to stop yourself in the middle of the overflow and initiate a search. This search should be to separate the immediate sources of irritation from older wounds. Often the search takes you back into childhood years when a similar situation contributed bad feelings to your reservoir. By tracing these old streambeds you can reduce the hostility focused on the present situation. By seeing *all* the sources of your bad feelings you can begin to solve the immediate problem. You can free yourself from the bondage of the past.

Another way to reduce the reservoir is to change your behavior. You can force yourself to act the healthy role. You can "assume the virtue". If you start acting less hostile you will begin to feel less hostile. This is because your emotions and actions tend to be consistent. If you wait until you feel good before you change your behavior you may have a long wait.

The reason for examining yourself is that the emotional foundations you possess as parents are the ones children are most likely to imitate. If you are burdened by repressed or consuming anger it is likely that your child will also. Modeling is so strong a force that it will be difficult to overcome the tendency for children to fill their reservoirs from yours. Clearly, the best remedy is to become healthier people and thereby become better models for children.

CHAPTER 7
COMMON ERRORS

Common Errors

Consistent parenting failures or mistakes can result in misbehavior, unmanageableness, and disruptiveness. It's easy to understand the presence of parenting failures from inadequate or incompetent parents. Gross problems such as parental neglect or abuse is expected to reflect adversely on children. But what of the normal, caring parents who find themselves with unmanageable children. Why is it that seemingly normal, stable families also produce problem children? Why might parents who show love and try hard to provide and guide children have significant problems with their kids?

Basically there are three types of errors made by normal families which account for many problems. *First,* the tool or tools (techniques) being used are inappropriate or ineffective. Craftsmen are familiar and skilled with the tools of the trade. Parents also need to be skilled with their tools and be able to switch to other techniques when necessary. Some parents simply redouble their efforts using the same incorrect technique. The result is frustration, anger, self-doubt, feelings of failure, and a multitude of self-recriminations. The problem is still present or a worse one develops.

Imagine the helpless parent who is trying his best yet achieves no results. Discouragement creeps in and negative expectations become prevalent. Once the bedraggled parent forms a negative expectation (expects failure), his child will live up to it. Chronic resentments are almost impossible to change because both sides look for failure. When the child makes a positive step forward, the parent, out of long-standing frustration, rejects the offer thereby rejuvenating the battle.

Remember, a technique is incorrect only because it is not getting the job done. Some techniques may not be the best for a particular problem, but they may get the job done reasonably well. That's OK. Here are some samples of goals and incorrect actions which lead to failure:

Goal   *Incorrect technique*

Independence —Child must always obtain approval before being allowed

Learn from
Mistakes   —Not allowing the child to fail; preventing a failure.

Respect For
Property
Rights   —Not allowing the child to "own" things.

Harmony between Sib-
lings   —Parents intercede in sibling conflict

Be Responsi-
ble   —Make all decisions for the child and ex-
                cuse the child from consequences.
Accept a "NO"
Answer   —Parent gives in to avoid an argument.
A *second* type of error is in the use of a specific technique. In sharpening a blade, for example, there is some
leeway for error in the angle of grinding. But, if the angle
leaves too narrow or too blunt a point then the blade will
not perform as well. The same principle exists in using a
particular child-rearing tool. There is some margin of
error that is acceptable, but too great a degree of change
in the technique may bring about failure. When you are
using the technique of Ignoring, but smile when your
child is showing off or telling a tall tale, then the technique may not work. If father is using the technique of
Consequences and has his child go to his room as isolation, but mother goes in and talks with the child, this also
may destroy the value of the technique. Know how to use
each tool correctly. Practice using each technique.

The *third* form of error is inconsistency. Once an
appropriate technique is selected and used correctly then
it must be given a real try. Sometimes a technique which
is not the best suited for a problem will work if used
consistently. A child who knows precisely what will happen as a result of his behavior will "test" less often. After
all, he knows what to expect. On the other hand, if he
doesn't know what will happen it's like gambling. Even if
the odds are against the child he may persist at gambling
to see what will occur. If you are consistent about daily
problems most difficulties will be alleviated within several weeks. Problems such as chores are often dramatically

changed within a week or two when your child knows what to expect and the proper technique is employed.

You may wonder how to tell when to switch to another technique because it is not working or persist at the technique until it works. Every situation is different so no precise guide is possible. As a general guideline, for daily chores if a technique is used properly and consistently (daily) for three weeks without any success then it is time to consider switching.

This book attempts to reduce parental error by describing each technique in detail, giving you advice as to the best technique for common situations, and providing ideas of how to employ the procedures to reach your goal.

Consistency

Most psychologists and child-rearing authorities agree on the importance of being consistent with discipline. Without consistency the result is unpredictable and the parent becomes a slot machine, dispensing rewards and punishments. The child cannot know whether he will be a winner or loser. In a child's world this means getting what he wants or getting frustrated by being deprived or punished. Life becomes a game of chance. And as in real life there will be many losers at the game. A loser is a child who keeps gambling, keeps playing the game. The child keeps playing because on the very next try he may win — get his way or escape a chore. In this game the parent loses because parents want to have their children stop playing the game — stop pushing.

Parents keep the game alive by being inconsistent. Why would a concerned parent continue this destructive inconsistency? There are several understandable reasons.

1. Parents want to be nice to their kids. Parents, therefore, avoid consistent punishment by giving in once in a while.
2. After saying "yes" or "no" several times there is a tendency to say the opposite. We try to be reasonable. We don't like to say "no" or "yes" all the time.
3. Parents get into habits of saying "yes" or more frequently "no" to requests. It is easier to say "no" than take the time to evaluate the request.
4. Parents are full of fears that something bad will happen to their children. Sometimes these fears become overpowering and a request will be granted or denied based only on underlying parental fear.
5. It is difficult to be consistent even in our own lives. Consequently, being consistent with children takes a lot of effort. Sometimes parents become understandably lax.
6. Being consistent may mean exerting effort at inconvenient times. Rounding up a child that escaped out the door before completing an assigned chore is an inconvenience. Habitually checking to see that a given chore is accomplished takes effort.
7. There are times that parents would rather do it themselves than hassle with the child. In the short run, the dishes get done faster, the house gets cleaned without the conflict if a parent goes ahead and tackles the job. Parents are tempted to avoid conflict with their children.

These above reasons for inconsistency are understandable for the parent, but not understandable to the child. All the child knows is that sometimes he gets out of doing a chore; sometimes he loses. Children, being very self centered, do not fully consider that they are getting their way at the expense of parental displeasure. Yet, even if children consider that their parents will be unhappy, self interest comes first.

It is difficult to exaggerate the importance of providing a consistent set of rules, consequences, and expectations. With the current state of knowledge about child-rearing many authorities are stressing consistency over such other issues as the degree of permissiveness or punishment. The trend is to say, however strict or lenient, harsh or benevolent, the key to having a healthier child is to be consistent with any policy.

A Permit to Misbehave — Warnings and Second Chances

Tommy: Bounce, bounce, bounce. ...

Mother: "Tommy, you know you're not to play with that ball in the living room."

Tommy: "Why not?" Bounce, bounce, bounce ...

Mother: "You're going to break something."

Tommy: Bounce, bounce, bounce ...

Mother: (Later) "Please stop throwing the ball — it's making me nervous."

Tommy: Bounce, bounce, bounce, ...

Mother: (Raising her voice) "Tommy, I asked you not to throw the ball!"

Tommy: Bounce, bounce, bounce, ...

Mother: (Louder) "I'm telling you for the last time not to throw the ball."

Tommy: (Waits 5 minutes, then) Bounce, bounce, bounce, ...

Mother: (Screaming) "OK young man, you do that once more and you spend the rest of the day in your room!"

Tommy: (Ignores it for a while)
Tommy: Bounce, bounce, bounce ...
Mother (Almost a scream but sounds determined) "Give
    me the ball and go to your room "
Tommy: "I'm sorry; I'll go outside and play."
Mother: (Trying to bring the matter to an end) "All right,
    but if you throw the ball in here again it's straight
    to your room."

While the above example might seem to be a slight exaggeration is not appreciably different from what occurs in most homes. The mother tried on seven different occasions to have Tommy comply with her wishes. She really tried to avoid punishing him and finally avoided sending him to his room when another alternative was offered. At another time she may have followed through with punishing him, but only after several warnings. You are left with the feeling that the next time Tommy bounces the ball in the living room he may or may not go straight to his room. He probably will get additional warnings.

From the mother's point of view there are several reasons for her giving warnings. She wants to be fair in giving Tommy a chance to straighten up; she may want to allow him to save face. Mother does not want to hear his pleadings or arguments when she sends him to his room. Moreover, she doesn't like to feel guilty for punishing her son. She would rather have him decide to be "good".

When mother's warnings fail to accomplish what she wants she becomes frustrated, irritated, and may lose her temper. She is disappointed that Tommy won't mind and feels helpless. Nevertheless, she continues to follow the same pattern of warnings.

Tommy, on the other hand, has learned something about the world around him. Although he may not have sat down and analyzed the situation he has learned that mother doesn't always mean what she says. He has learned that he can irritate mother without a negative consequence. He has been given, in effect, a permit to misbehave. It's mighty like getting an extension on your tax bill without having to pay any penalty. And, you may even get out of paying taxes altogether. Kind of worth the battle with those odds, isn't it?

Tommy has learned that every once in a while he gets immediately into trouble, especially when mother isn't feeling well. But that's only once in a while. With each new event he expects to get a new warning and will resent it if mother follows through with promised threats. He learned to ignore mother which is the first step toward ignoring anyone in authority. In his effort to test out how far he can push he may go far beyond his real intent. He is learning to have little respect for authority.

To avoid the error of giving your child extra rope (second chances) in which to further misbehave, you may want to give warnings only under the following situations:

1. When your child could not have known what he did was wrong. A very young child may put water in the gas tank to "help" his father. This is not malicious and a firm statement with an explanation is appropriate.

2. With conscientious children who normally do what is expected, an occasional second chance is reasonable. There *is* such a thing as forgetting, especially if it is a minor and infrequent mistake. In cases where your child has forgotten and forgetting is not the child's usual way of avoiding responsibil-

ities, then a warning is reasonable.

3. With infrequent situations you will not disturb anything if a warning, threat, or second chance is given. By infrequent situation I mean that warnings should probably not be given more than once or twice a month.

A permit to misbehave is granted by you in the hopes of having your child correct himself. If those hopes are not met, if your child does not jump in and comply, then the second chance is like giving a permit to repeat the original mistake. Another aspect of warnings is that they have a tendency to shift the burden of responsibility back on you. You are the one who needs to faithfully check. Repetitive warnings result in the child learning to rely on you for reminders. Part of taking responsibility is to remind oneself and pay the consequence for forgetting. The simple conclusion and solution is to avoid reminders and second warnings. Stop issuing permits to misbehave.

Home Traffic Officer

Parents can easily fall into the role of a traffic officer around the house. You resolve kids' arguments by punishing them, taking sides, or directing them away from the argument. Breaking up the argument, fight or bickering is done in the name of peace and quiet. Your desire is to have the kids get along without the fighting.

"If you don't stop fighting _____!" That phrase is frequently echoed in homes throughout the land. Examples of threatened consequences are:

... you'll go to your room and stay there the rest of the day.

... you're both going to get it.

187

... I'll take away the cards (or whatever is being argued about).

Still other variations involve appeals to the child's sense of shame: "Why can't you two play in peace?" Parents may send the bickering pair outside or determine who is at fault and assign ample punishment.

Hopefully you can see that as with other warnings and threats the traffic officer role will lead to frustration. Do children stop their fighting or arguing? Sometimes, for the moment. Actually, that quiet period, after your threat, accomplishes the opposite of what you want. It teases you into believing that your threat is necessary and effective — after all, it worked. Didn't it? The truth is that it accomplished two things which you don't want to have happen. It fools you into believing a home traffic officer is necessary. It is not necessary. You can accomplish your goals without threats and often without your intervention. There are other, easier ways to handle these situations. The other tendency you don't want to have happen is that your children learn to ignore you until you threaten them. They depend upon you to settle conflicts, set limits, and direct their lives. This practice robs the kids of resolving their own squabbles, imposing self-limits, and taking responsibility for their own lives. The kids pressure you back into the traffic officer role even when you want to change.

The traffic officer does more than settle sibling conflicts. He or she is the center of the family universe. All roads lead to this person. Typically it is the mother that assumes this chore but it could be a father. Below is a picture of how the home traffic officer might function.

As you can see, all communications go through the central parent. The spouse speaks through the traffic officer if he/she wants to communicate with the children. The problems involved in this system are enormous for the family as well as the central parent. Here are a list of pitfalls for the traffic officer and family:

1. Misunderstandings arise because some family members don't talk directly.
2. The traffic officer can't help but distort some communications, regardless of the well-intentions.
3. When people resolve conflicts directly they grow closer and form warm relationships. An intermediary interferes in the process and destroys potential closeness.
4. The traffic officer carries a heavy burden. He/She is called upon to smooth things over. The threat is that if there are problems it becomes the traffic officer's fault.
5. The traffic officer is sucked into every family conflict. There's never any rest. The person is frantic and overwhelmed with all the family problems.
6. Usually people get angry at the traffic officer because problems are unresolved despite all efforts. Sometimes the traffic officer doesn't have control over the problem.
7. Resentment and frustration are felt by the home

traffic officer because that person gets the blame without the credit.

8. It is a horribly confining role. The officer becomes so attached and identified with this role that it stifles independence. If parents abandon the traffic officer role they may be afraid there won't be any role for them in the family. They won't be needed.

A more open family network encourages independence and free communication. A picture of this arrangement might look like this:

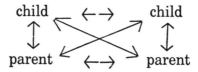

Each parent and child share the responsibility for communicating and problem solving. The burden is distributed more evenly. The traffic officer backs off, allowing others to negotiate, confront, and resolve issues. This family arrangement is much healthier for everyone.

How can a parent or family change their pattern? How can an open network be established? Let's return to the example of a home traffic officer managing the children and see how change can take place.

When the kids argue the home traffic officer would give warnings, threats or mediate the situation. The simple solution and the one which works best is to have the parent ignore children's arguments. Bite your tongue if necessary, remove yourself, or remove the children from your presence. Is this a safe policy? Yes!

As was stated earlier there are *rare* families when one child deliberately inflicts severe harm on another. You need to become involved when severe damage is imminent. The likelihood of one child really hitting another in the head with a hammer, cutting the other up, or inflicting severe deliberate damage is rare! From the yells and screams it may seem that's what is happening, but it is play acting. If you are one of those rare families you should consult a professional.

Unbelievable as it sounds, without parental interference children will eventually work out their own arguments and settle their own battles. The big kids will learn that they shouldn't slug too hard because they inflict too much pain. The smaller ones learn just how far to bait the stronger ones before getting hurt.

One of the first things a reformed home traffic officer will observe is that the children will come to them to settle battles or to gain support. Be prepared against being drawn into children's arguments. What can be said to a tearful, pleading, pathetic 5-year-old when he seeks your protection from his tough 9-year-old sibling who just took away a toy? That rascal of an older brother is holding the toy in front of you. Dear parent, put your police badge down and give a sympathetic ear to the younger child. Let him know that you understand his anger by voicing how *he* feels (cheated, taken advantage of, etc.). Nevertheless, you make it clear that he has to fight his own battles. Most times this can be done by just not jumping to his rescue. Be understanding by using Reflective Listening, *nothing else.*

This policy does work if maintained consistently. It will save on your nerves and allow your children to tackle problems by themselves. They no longer need to have mommy or daddy intervene.

The reformed home traffic officer has to confront a spouse who expects that you carry out his/her wishes. The spouse may want you to, "Tell the kids_____," or, "Have the kids do_____". Likewise the reformed officer hears the children say, "Please ask daddy if I can go out to-night." Or, the child tries to enlist your sympathy by saying that the other parent is unfair.

The best policy for the reformed traffic officer is to remove oneself as the messenger and arbitrator. You can accomplish this by the use of Reflective Listening, an announcement that "You'll have to work that out with him/her" and diligence in keeping out of the center. It won't be easy because the family expects you to do every-thing and will resist the change. Within a matter of a month you ought to see some positive changes but be prepared for setbacks and family turmoil. In the long run your efforts will be rewarded.

Control

What amount of control is best to have over your child's activities? The question is obviously difficult to answer. It has been this author's observation that many parents who attempt to exert the most control are the least effective in gaining control. That sounds like a sweeping generalization and perhaps it is. Still, many families are in an uproar with parents loudly demanding respect and obedience while the children are disrespectful and disobedient.

One reason for the dilemma is that it is difficult to be consistent with a multitude of controls. The more activi-

___

ties you want to control or direct, the more opportunity for inconsistency. If you make 20 requests in a day then you need to be consistent and follow through with 20 consequences. "Don't touch that." "Pick up your toys." "Come here." "Help me with this." "Stop doing that." These are all commands, situations where you are seeking control. If your child is slow or does not respond to one third of the commands, then you have about 7 confrontations to respond to and be consistent about. If you tend to be inconsistent and lax in enforcement then your child will challenge more and more of your commands. Clearly, this leads to a frustrating, overwhelming day.

If you were only to give a third as many commands, say 7, then you might have about two confrontations in a day. By handling the two situations with appropriate consequences your child will be less disagreeable and more obedient in the future. Remember the saying of too many cooks in the kitchen and the soup is spoiled. Well, too many commands spoil parent-child relationships. But, you may ask, how can you avoid all those commands when Freddy constantly gets into mischief, disobeys, or refuses to do his work? A logical response is, what you are attempting to do didn't work anyway so you need to do something different. Below are a few of the alternatives you can choose from:

ignore it	wear ear plugs
tolerate it	cry
hope for the best	go tell a neighbor
bite your tongue	do it yourself
go to another room	put the child up for adoption

Seriously, you need to find other ways of coping without issuing commands that you cannot back up. You need to start by doing a few things well, have them in control before expanding. You have years in which to expand the number of controls or demands. Issuing too many all at once will not get the job done and it will be torture on you besides.

Control tends to be most effective when a youngster *knows* that his parents will follow through on *each* demand or instruction. He does not think to test the control because the control has been very consistent in the past. So, again, start out with only those requests or rules you will doggedly enforce. Let loose, temporarily, with all those requests and rules which are haphazardly enforced. If you have a good track record of maintaining control (checking and enforcing the consequences) then it will be much easier to add new requests and chores.

Having fewer commands which are enforced leads to more compliance from children. The more compliance the better you feel and the more positive you will act toward your children. Positive feelings and expectations are reinforcing and build a better relationship. The result is that you can attain more compliance, a friendlier relationship, and less arguments by beginning with fewer commands or rules that you can enforce.

CHAPTER 8
DEVELOPMENTAL
TIMETABLE

Child Rearing: What To Do Now

Developmental Timetable

Setting a timetable of do's and don'ts is a difficult proposition in child-rearing. Children vary enormously while still falling within acceptable limits. There are many excellent developmental timetables for infants and toddlers. You may want to consult or purchase several and refer to them from time to time.

A summary of important points to consider and tasks to implement are presented in the developmental schedule which follows:

Age	Concept	Explanation of the concept and action plan
0-1	Stimulation	Starting immediately after birth begin holding, rubbing, fondling, stroking, and carrying the infant. Provide lots of stimulation. In the first year,

changes of visual and sound cues such as mobiles, color patterns, noises and music help provide the needed varying stimulation. Stimulate all the senses: smell, touch, textures, balance, taste, etc. Keep handy a variety of objects that can be put in the infant's hands, in front of its face, and in its mouth. *Don't* make the infant's environment boring! Avoid putting an infant in a hard carrier for long periods of time. Movement is very important so get into the habit of carrying the infant about in a sling or appropriate back pack.

0-1	Talk	Several important long-term investigations have concluded that talking to infants is of immense value. Talking does provide stimulation. It also provides a tremendous boost in language development. Don't be afraid to "baby talk" but you should also use adult language. Get into the habit of telling your child what you are doing. "I am going to change your diapers. You first need to lie down. Here is the safety pin.

Off comes the diaper. My gosh, it's wet! Here is a dry, fresh diaper." The more talking you do the better it will be for your child. It is incredible how much an infant can perceive. You may even want to read to your infant. Make it something you are interested in so you can read for a comfortably long time.

0-1   Learning   The principal form of learning you should be concerned with at this stage is imitation or modeling. Imitate the infant's sounds and movements and encourage your infant to imitate you. Move the infant's arms, legs and head to imitate your movements. Make all the sounds and noises of objects around the environment such as trains, horns, sirens, falling water and the wind.

0-1   Attention   There is some controversy as to when you should begin to ignore attention-getting crying or fussing. Some experts suggest that excess crying can be controlled by the moderate use of Ignoring techniques. Other experts suggest that it is healthier for the infant to be held whenever he begins to cry. A middle ground might be to make some change in the infant's environment such as introducing a noise, sound, light or light variation, or a new body position rather than *always* picking your infant up and comforting him. Infants will cry out of boredom as well as from discomfort. Varying the environment reduces boredom and crying. Don't be afraid to ignore your infant's excessive crying. You need to give yourself a break also.

1-2   Stimulation   Continue varying the environment. If you use a playpen, make sure there are lots of different things in it.

1-2   Talk   There is an amazing transition during this year in language development. Continue talking to your child with or without any response. Begin a regular reading schedule. As learning occurs, have the child pronounce the words rather than grunt, squeal, gesture, whine, or point to the needed thing. By the end of the second

		year the words "please" and "thank you" should be commonplace in your child's language.
1-2	Learning	Self-help skills can be started in this year. Have your child begin to assist in dressing and particularly undressing. Praise the child for movements in the right direction. Continue imitating and encouraging imitation. Allow trial-and-error learning to take place. This means allow some degree of failure.
1-2	Chores	Your child should begin to help with meal preparation, serving, and clean-up. The tasks may be small but emphasize the contribution. Praise efforts in the right direction. Some help can be expected toward putting away toys. "Let's pick up these toys together!" In an excited and positive voice you can also say,"Let's see how fast we can pick up each toy!"
1-2	Property	Begin identifying the child's personal property. Objects such as a toothbrush, comb and brush may now be described as the child's.

2-3	Stimulation	"Where is *your* toothbrush?" Let your child wander as freely about as possible. "Child proof" the house so you don't have to confine the child to certain areas.
2-3	Talk	Have regular reading times. Begin introducing various memory and comprehension exercises. "How many numbers (letters) can you remember?" "What did I just hide that was on the table?" "What word did I leave out from the story?" "Repeat as much of the story as you can remember."
2-3	Learning	Bathroom routine becomes habit during this year. Such other self-help skills as dressing and feeding are nearly completed. Allow your child to do the work rather than you struggling with dressing and feeding. Praise the efforts and success repeatedly.
2-3	Chores	More than one command or instruction can be given at one time. "Helping" is stressed and praised. Make it fun to help or

work. The child should have regular work assignments but should not be expected to do the job without reminders.

2-3	Social	Valuable skills such as waiting your turn, Interaction and sharing emerge. Stress how good it is to take turns. "Mother will share her peaches with Billy. Does Billy want to share his peas with Mother? Oh, Billy is so generous to share his peas with Mother. Thank you Billy." Ignore inappropriate attention-getters such as whining, crying, and temper tantrums.
3-4	Learning	Tiolet training should be completed but delays are normal. Dressing self should be accomplished without help. You should allow lots of "learn from experience" situations. Avoid saying "no", "Don't do that", or "Stop that".
3-4	Chores	A child's first long-term responsibility is given. It could be setting the table. Make your child feel that the job is important and that his work is valued. Bedtime rules may need to be formulated if that is a prob-

		lem.
3-4	Personal Property	The child should be accustomed to "owning" property. If you use his property, get permission. This shows that you respect and honor your child.
3-4	Social	Your child will be seeking attention through language. "Why?" questions are asked but not necessarily because of wanting to know why. Let the child capture 100% of your attention if it is done appropriately. Reduce the duration rather than the percentage of attention. Five minutes of 100% attention is better than 15 minutes of 50% attention. It's the quality, not quantity. Inappropriate attention-getters are ignored. Make sure the child has periods of time to be alone. Increase the time alone over the next several years.
4-5	Chores	You will want to increase the number and/or complexity of chores. Avoid reminders and threats.
4-5	Social	Encourage the independence of going off to play with others. Overnight visits with friends and relatives is a good idea.

		Nursery school is also a good way to increase social interaction.
5-7	Chores	Your child should have several independent responsibilities which are now habits. Encourage the child to put away his own things. Allow as much responsibilities and independence as the child requests (as long as it is safe). Maintain a "you can do it if you satisfy my (parental) requirements (of supervision, safety, etc.)". Ignore attitude; stick to targets.
5-7	Education	Place emphasis on and interest in schooling. Ask, "What did you learn in school today?" Show that interest on a daily basis. This is the way you convey that you value education. Make sure homework is completed. Talk with the teacher several times a year, beginning early in the school term. You may want to augment regular education with an older "tutor" or provide a special music, art, or other skill class.
8-18	Parent/ Child	The foundation has already been laid.. If it is not a good foundation you have problems!

Your role now shifts to being a Reflective Listener. Rules are kept to a minimum. Encourage your child to find ways in which everyone's needs can be met — through Negotiation. Attempt to remedy situations through praise and encouragement rather than by punishment and negativism. Education is stressed by seeing samples of the child's work, setting aside time for homework, praising academic accomplishment, meeting regularly with teachers, and visiting the library to obtain books. Your child's education is *your* responsibility.

As you can tell from the above descriptions, several factors transcend ages. They are: praise and positive attention for desirable behavior; freedom for the child to make mistakes and fail; and responsibilities have consequences which are consistently enforced.

CHAPTER 9
EDUCATION AND
SCHOOLING

Child Rearing: What To Do Now

208

Readiness skills

Readiness means that necessary skills must be developed/learned/practiced before other advanced skills are possible. There are prerequisites to the basic 3 R's which parents are responsible for. Before nursery school, you should work with your child on language skills, understanding numbers, fine motor and gross motor development. Obtain help from teachers or the school district to assist you in this task. You should be checking for hearing and vision impairments. Are there any physical handicaps?

Ask teachers, librarians, college professors (early child development, education, special education departments, or child psychology), or school psychologists for help in obtaining good developmental schedules. Bookstores are beginning to have more of these works on the shelves, so visit large bookstores. Consult with nursery schools or kindergarten teachers about what skills children are expected to have before entering the class. Ask them for exercises in developing skills which your child lacks.

One of the best preparations for school is for parents to make learning fun and exciting. Reward, with your attention and praise, the child's efforts toward education. Show interest in what children learn. Having young children accustomed to playing with other children, taking orders from other adults, persistence at entertaining themselves, and not being in need of constant adult attention are all factors which provide for an easier transition to classrooms.

Teachers and classrooms

Nursery schools are good training and observing grounds. If your child is not fully comfortable with other children and adults it may be a good idea to try a nursery school. This will get youngsters into the routine of "school". You should visit the nursery school and spend at least 3 to 4 hours in observing the school before enrolling the child. Ask other parents what experience they have had with the school.

Start your career in parent-teacher discussions early. Teachers may not volunteer information, so ask questions What are some of the questions? You need to know if there are social or academic deficiencies. Are behavioral problems interfering with the child's concentration? At the nursery school age, there are several points to review with the teacher:

1. Can the child take directions? Is the child difficult to work with? Does he act up to get attention? Will

he follow orders?
2. What is the frustration level? Can he sit still and work or play for reasonable periods of time? How is anger handled?
3. How does he get along with playmates? Does he generally cooperate and make friends?
4. Is he happy? Does he like school?

By having regular parent-teacher conferences you can catch problems early. Spend time observing at the school. See for yourself what is going on and how your child works and plays. By observing in the school, you can compare your child with other children of about the same age.

The same basic questions and procedures are followed in kindergarten. Consult with the teacher at least four times in the kindergarten year, more if there is a problem. Make the first contact when school begins. No problems mean briefer discussions. You still need to ask the questions rather than waiting for the teacher to volunteer.

Teachers are careful about what they tell parents. Making the teacher relaxed and at ease will loosen his tongue (they are people like the rest of us). Visiting and talking with a teacher demonstrates your concern in your child and his education. Usually, teachers will respond to parental concern by (consciously or unconsiously) "favoring" your child, putting more effort into your child's education, and contacting you whenever there is a problem.

Ask teachers if they forsee any future problems, academically or socially for your child. Find out what your child's strengths are. You will want to work on the strengths through praise or extra training as well as the deficiencies.

If your child doesn't like a nursery school or kindergarten teacher find out why. Observe the problem in class. If your child has a poor or incompetent teacher in one of the first few years of school, it can result in a poor academic start and/or a "turned-off" child. If the problem is the teacher, what can be done? You can talk to the teacher and if necessary the principal, the school superintendent and ultimately the School Board. If you are convinced that the teacher is the problem, ask for a change in classes (Teachers). Don't settle for, "It's the policy" or "It can't be done" answer. If you are unable to obtain satisfaction with one level of administration go to the higher one. The final and rather drastic step may be to take your child out of school. This forces the school to take action. If the school pursues legal action you can have your day in court. If you have a reasonable case against the teacher, you can legally force the school into making a change. Schools will avoid major confrontations. They don't want to waste time in court battling a concerned parent! (Being illegal, it is not proper to advise against sending your child to school. If a parent contemplates such a measure he should consult legal assistance.)

The strong and assertive position mentioned above is fortunately not needed very often. It is a rare situation where an elementary school teacher is incompetent. Far and away the problem that results in children disliking a teacher is a home problem. An example of what is meant is a child who is accustomed to getting his way at home. The child gets angry at the teacher when he cannot get his selfish way or when he is corrected. The teacher cannot be faulted for an inadequate child-rearing program at home.

In summary, teachers are there to help you educate your child. Take advantage of their observations, suggestions, and knowledge of your child. Don't allow them to be strangers.

Academics

How reliable and valid are school grades and so-called standardized tests? Tests and grades can provide you with a treasury of information. Let's review some situations. Grades in many elementary schools are often rated as satisfactory or unsatisfactory performance. Junior and senior high schools generally retained the "A", "B", "C" form of grading. Are your child's grades all consistently low? If they are all low , what are the alternative explanations? There are usually two reasons for low ("D" and "F") grades: an undetected learning disability and a behavioral problem.

Learning disability. The term learning disability covers a large array of handicaps. Some handicaps can be traced to visual or auditory deficiencies. A simple eye-chart test may uncover vision deficiencies. A thorough vision and hearing test is a must. Don't wait and assume everything is fine.

If there is a consistent pattern of poor performance overall or in certain subjects you can request, through the teacher, that your child be tested by the school psychologist. This is your right under the law so don't be afraid to request it. A school psychologist should be able to determine if there is a learning disability and what type. The school psychologist can also determine if the problem is other than a learning disability; it could be a behavior problem, poor attention, daydreaming, lazy, or another emotional problem. The school psychologist should meet with you and review the findings. If the school psychologist doesn't make an appointment with you then you take the initiative. You will want to know the following items:

1. A detailed description of the problem. A school psychologist will be able to explain the problem in simple, understandable language; they are trained to do this. So, if they are using words and concepts you cannot understand, ask the person to translate it into language you can understand. Write down each point in order for you to remember what is said. The school psychologist may not tell you exact scores on specific tests but he/she will give you a good picture of the range of performance. Spend as much time as you need to completely understand the situation. You need information and the school psychologist is the expert. You can learn from that person what you need to know about your child.

2. What can the school do to remedy the situation? The school psychologist will be able to develop an individualized program to remedy most deficits in the same way a physician will give you a prescription for an illness. Part of this prescriptive program may be carried out in school. Find out what that program is. It may be a set of academic or behavioral exercises, a special class, or a change in classes. Keep a record of exactly what the school intends to do about the problem. Make sure you see the connection between the problem and the prescriptive program.

3. What can you do at home to remedy the situation?

School personnel forget that parents can be excellent aids. You may need to specifically ask what you can do to help. Your options include: providing programmed exercises, making sure homework is completed, being a listener for reading assignments, hiring a tutor, or supplementing the school work with additional assignments.

4. Is a referral for other help in order? There is a large array of personnel within and outside the school that can be utilized, if necessary. There are speech pathologists and language specialists, visual and auditory specialists, clinical psychologists, learning disabilities experts, and diagnostic institutes. Ask if a referral is in order.

The reason for keeping a record of your visit with the school psychologist is threefold: you're likely to forget many details; you will want to use the material when you talk with the teacher(s); and you'll want to check periodically to make sure the school is doing what they "promised".

Behavioral Problems. As with learning disability, behavioral problems can mean many things. Misbehavior, inattention, withdrawal, anger, impulse control, a demanding nature or shyness are all sources of low grades. With help from teachers and school psychologists in identifying the sources of low grades, you can remedy behavioral problems with the principles given in this book.